Date Due

NEW CRITICAL ESSAYS

Also by Roland Barthes

═══════════
═══════════

Roland Barthes

NEW
CRITICAL
ESSAYS

Translated by
Richard Howard

HILL AND WANG   NEW YORK

A division of Farrar, Straus and Giroux

Translation copyright © 1980 by Farrar, Straus and Giroux, Inc.
Originally published in French as
Le degré zéro de l'écriture suivi de Nouveaux essais critiques,
© Editions du Seuil 1972   All rights reserved
Published simultaneously in Canada by McGraw-Hill Ryerson
Ltd., Toronto
Printed in the United States of America
Designed by Jeffrey Schaire

Library of Congress Cataloging in Publication Data
Barthes, Roland.   New critical essays.
Translation of Nouveaux essais critiques,
published in 1972 as the second part of a volume
of which Le degré zéro de l'écriture was the first part.
Contents:
La Rochefoucauld: "Reflections, or Sentences and maxims."
The plates of the Encyclopedia.
Chauteaubriand: life of Rancé. [etc.]
1. French literature
History and criticism
Collected works.
I. Title.
PQ139.B3213   840'.9   80–12345
ISBN 0–8090–7257–2

Contents

NEW CRITICAL ESSAYS

La Rochefoucauld:
"Reflections
or Sentences and Maxims"

There are two ways to read La Rochefoucauld: by citing, or straight through. In the first case, I open the book from time to time, select a *pensée*, savor its suitability, appropriate it to my own circumstance—I make this anonymous form into the very voice of my situation or of my mood; in the second case, I read the maxims in sequence, like a narrative or an essay; but then the book scarcely concerns *me*—La Rochefoucauld's maxims are so repetitive that they reveal their author, his obsessions, and his age, but not ourselves. So that the same work, read in different ways, seems to contain two contradictory projects: on the one hand, a *for-me* (and what an aim! This particular maxim traverses three centuries to land on target, to tell about *me!*); on the other, a *for-itself*, something of the author's which speaks, repeats, imposes itself as though caught up in an endless, chaotic discourse, a kind of obsessive monologue.

These two readings are not, however, contradictory, because in the collection of maxims the broken discourse remains an enclosed discourse; of course, materially, I must choose between reading the maxims selectively or in sequence, and the effect of this will be contrary—here brilliant, there stifling; but the very fruit of the work's discontinuity and disorder is that each maxim is, in a sense, the archetype of all; the maxims have a structure which is both unique and varied; in other words, to a critique of development, of composition, of evolution, and even of continuity, we might prefer a critique of the sentence's unity, of its contour, in short, of its form: it is always to the maxim that we must return, and not to the maxims.

But first of all, with regard to this structure—are there maxims which don't have it? In other words, are there maxims which are formally free, as we say there is *free verse?* Such maxims do exist, and in La Rochefoucauld himself, but they are no longer called maxims—they are *Reflections.* Such reflections are fragments of discourse, *texts* without structure, without spectacle; through them, it is once more a fluid, continuous language, i.e., just the opposite of that extremely archaic verbal order which governs the maxim's contour. In principle, La Rochefoucauld did not include his *Reflections* in the *corpus* of his maxims (although they bear on the same subjects), for what is involved here is a different literature altogether; yet we shall find some maxims exempt from structure: this is precisely because, without yet taking up much space, they have already abandoned the sentential order, they are on the way toward the Reflection, i.e., toward discourse. When we read:

> We cannot love except in relation to ourselves, and merely follow our taste and our inclination when we prefer our friends to ourselves; yet it is by this preference alone that friendship can be genuine and perfect . . .

we realize that we are in an order of language which is no longer that of the maxim; something is missing, which is the *stamp,* the very spectacle of utterance, what we might call, in short, the citation; but also something else is present, to which the maxim itself has not accustomed us: a certain fragility, a certain discursive caution, a language more delicate, more open to kindliness, as if, conversely, the maxim could only be mean—as if the closure of the maxim were also a closing of the heart. Thus there are, in La Rochefoucauld's work, certain *open* maxims, certain maxims-as-discourse (however brief): these are not, generally, the ones we cite, for in them no hook *catches;* they are merely the good housewives of discourse; the others reign there as goddesses.

As for these others, in fact, the structure is there, confining sensibility, effusion, scruple, hesitation, regret, persuasion, too, within a castrating mechanism. The maxim is a hard, shiny—and fragile—object, like an insect's thorax; like an insect, too, the maxim possesses a sting, that hook of sharp-pointed words which conclude and crown it—which close it even as they arm it (the maxim is armed *because* it is closed). What does this structure consist of? Of certain stable elements quite independent of grammar, united by a fixed relation which, again, owes nothing to syntax.

Not only is the maxim a proposition severed from discourse, but inside this very proposition there reigns, further, a subtler discontinuity; a normal sentence, a *spoken* sentence always tends to dissolve its parts into each other, to equalize the flux of thought; it progresses, in short, according to an apparently unorganized process; in the maxim, the converse is the case; the maxim is a general unit composed of particular units; the skeleton—and bones are hard things—is more than apparent: spectacular. The whole of the maxim's structure is visible, precisely insofar as it is erratic. What are these internal units which support the maxim's architecture? Not what are usually the liveliest parts of the sentence, the relations, but on the contrary the motionless, solitary parts, we might call them essences, which are usually substantives but occasionally adjectives or verbals as well, each of which refers to a complete, eternal, in fact autarchic meaning: *love, passion, pride, wound, deceive, delicate, impatient,* such are the closed meanings on which the maxim is constructed. What defines these formal essences is doubtless, in the last analysis, that they are the *terms* (the *relata*) of a relation (of comparison or of antithesis); but this relation is much less apparent than its constituents; in the maxim, the intellect first perceives certain complete substances, not the gradual flux of the thought. If I read: "Everyone complains of his own memory, and no one of his own judgment," my mind is struck by the plenitude of these solitary terms: *memory, judgment, complains;* and since, in spite of everything, these star words stand out against a certain more modest background, I have the (profoundly aesthetic) sense that I am dealing with a veritable *metrical* economy of thought, distributed within the fixed and finite space which is imparted to it (the length of a maxim) in strong beats (the substances, the essences) and in weak beats (tool words, relational words); easy to recognize in this economy a substitute for the versified languages: there is, as we know, a special affinity between verse and maxim, between aphoristic and divinatory communication.

And just as verse is essentially a *measured* language, so the strong beats of a maxim are captives of a number: we have maxims with two, three, four, five, or seven beats, according to the number of semantic accents. If I read: "Self-love is the greatest of all flatterers," the relation of identity designates only two strong beats for me *(self-love* and *flatterers);* but if I read: "Men's happiness and misery depend less on their disposition than on fortune," it is evident that I am dealing with a four-beat maxim. These numbers are not of equal importance; every maxim obviously tends, according to the canon of classical art, toward antiphrasis, i.e., toward symmetry; hence it is the even meters (we are concerned here with "semantic" meters) which saturate the maxim most naturally. The quaternary meter is doubtless the most accomplished, for it permits the development of a proportion, i.e., both a harmony and a complexity; examples of it are numerous in La Rochefoucauld, based rhetorically on metaphor; we have maxims like: "Rank is to merit what finery is to handsome persons," in which the four strong terms are linked together by a relationship of compensation. This is a privileged example of binary economy; but the other types of maxims, despite appearances, always return, as it happens, to a two-term organization; this is the case for all the maxims having an odd number of strong beats; for in these maxims, the odd term always has an eccentric function; it remains external to the even structure and merely tops it; if I read: "It requires greater virtues to withstand good luck than bad," it is clear that there are three strong beats (*virtues, good luck, bad luck;* but these three terms do not receive the same accent: the last two (*good luck* and *bad*) form the veritable pillars of the relation (they serve to construct an antithesis), while the first term *(virtues)* is, in fact, no more than the general reference with regard to which the relation becomes significative. This odd term (the same is true of maxims with five or seven beats) has, therefore, a singular function, simultaneously general, distant, and yet fundamental; in the old logic, we would say that it is the *subject* of the maxim (that of which it speaks), whereas the even terms are its predicate (what is said of the subject); in modern logic, it is rather what we call a *circuit of signification,* i.e., the referential class of objects within which the confrontation of certain characteristics is not absurd: for according to the maxim's momentary truth, the opposition of good and bad luck is somehow valid only with regard to the virtues. Hence the odd term occupies a place sufficiently eccentric for the maxim's structure, in the long run, to be always even—i.e., binary, since by being even, the terms of the relation can always be distributed into two opposing groups.

This stubbornly dual character of the maxim's structure is important, for it governs the relation which unites its terms;

this relation is dependent upon the strength, the rarity, and the parity of the beats which it links together. When a language—and this is the case for maxims—proposes several strong-beat, essential terms, it is inevitable that the relation be absorbed into them: the stronger the substantives, the more the relation tends to immobility. Indeed, if two strong objects (I mean, psychological objects), for example, *sincerity* and *dissimulation*, are presented, the relation which spontaneously develops between them always tends to be a motionless one of manifestation, i.e., of equivalence: sincerity is (or is not) equivalent to dissimulation: the very power of the terms, their solitude, their *luster*, permit virtually no other relationship, whatever their terminological variations. We are confronted, then, by the very state of the maxim's structure with a relation of essence not of *praxis*, of identity not of transformation; in effect, the language of the maxim always has a definitional and not a transitive activity; a collection of maxims is always more or less (and this is flagrant in La Rochefoucauld) a dictionary, not a book of recipes: it illuminates the being of certain kinds of behavior, not their modes or their techniques. This relation of equivalence is of a rather archaic type: to define things (with the help of a motionless relation) is always more or less to make them sacred, and the maxim does not fail to do so, despite its rationalistic project.

Hence the maxim is very generally subject to a relation of equivalence: one term is (or is not) *worth* the other. The most elementary state of this relation is purely comparative: the maxim confronts two objects with each other, for instance, *strength* and *will*, and is content to posit their quantitative relation: *We have more strength than will;* this movement is the source of a good number of maxims. Here we find the three degrees of comparison: *more, as much as, less;* but since the maxim chiefly subserves a project of denunciation, it is obviously the critical comparatives which prevail: the maxim tells us that there is *more* passion in this or that virtue than we suppose: that is its habitual enterprise. As we see, this enterprise, if we choose to psychoanalyze its structure for a moment, is based entirely on an imagination of weight; like a god, the author of the maxims hefts certain objects and tells us their actual weight; to weigh is, in fact, a divine activity, as a whole —and very ancient—iconography testifies. But La Rochefoucauld is not a god; his thought, resulting from a rationalist movement, remains profane: he never weighs a singular and metaphysical Fault, but only faults, plural and temporal: he is a chemist, not a priest (but we also know that in our collective imagination the divine theme and the scientific theme remain very close).

Above the comparative state comes the second state of the relation of equivalence: identity; this is doubtless a more nearly closed, a *riper* state, since here we are not content to present and confront two objects in order to infer thereby a clumsily quantitative relation; we define this relation in essence, no longer in quantity; we posit that *this* is *that,* by substance and for eternity, that *moderation is a form of fear,* that *self-love is a flatterer,* that *envy is a passion,* etc. These are examples of simple, quite homogeneous identities, arranged like a regular progress of essences in a world of motionless truth. But sometimes, too, equivalence is more emphatic: *We do not yield (to those more powerful than we are) for the advantage we want to give,* La Rochefoucauld says, *but for the advantage we want to gain;* thus the positive proposition *(the advantage we want to gain)* is reinforced by the very representation of its contrary *(the advantage we want to give);* it is this simultaneously opposed and convergent movement that we find in maxims which appear anything but egalitarian: "Men would not live long in society if they were not duped by each other;" which actually means: men are duped by each other, otherwise they would not live in society.

But the most significative relation, the one which might pass for the very model of the Rochefoucauldian maxim, is the relation of a demystifying identity, whose ordinary expression is the restrictive copula: *is only.* "The clemency of princes is often only a policy to gain the affection of the people . . ." or again: "The sage's constancy is only the art of keeping his agitation shut up within his heart;" examples here are abundant and clear; in them we readily recognize what would today be called a debunking relation, since the author, by a single word, reduces the appearance *(clemency, constancy)* to its reality *(a policy, an art). Is only* is in short the maxim's key word, for we are not concerned here with a simple disclosure (which is sometimes indicated by the expression *in effect,* with the meaning: *in reality*); this disclosure is almost always reductive; it does not explain, it defines the more (the appearance) by the less (the reality).[1] We might be tempted to make this degrading relation (since it demotes appearance for the sake of an always less glorious reality) into the logical expression of what has been called La Rouchefoucauld's pessimism; doubtless the restriction, especially if it starts from the virtues to end with the accidents and passions, is not euphoric: in appearance it is an avaricious, constrained movement, it corrodes the generosity of the world, and its diversity as well; but this pessimism is ambiguous; it is also the fruit of a thirst, if not for explication, at least for explicitation; it participates in a certain disillusion, no doubt, consonant with the author's aristocratic situation; but also, surely, in a positive impulse of rationalization, of the integration of disparate elements: La Rochefoucauld's vision is not dialectical, and for that reason it is

---

[1]Oddly enough, if the *if only* is indeed demystifying in the order of essences, it becomes mystifying in the order of praxis. *One need only . . .* is the expression charged with assurance, illusion, and absurdity used by every armchair general.

a despairing one; but it is rationalistic, and for that reason, like every philosophy of clarity, it is progressive; copying La Rochefoucauld himself, we might say in the restrictive form so dear to him: La Rochefoucauld's pessimism is only an incomplete rationalism.

Once the terms and the relation of the maxim are described, has its form been exhausted? Not at all. It is a mistake, I believe, to impute only two levels to a work: that of form and that of content; form itself can include several levels: structure, as we have seen, is one of these; but we have also seen that in order to gain access to this structure, it was necessary to disengage the maxim from its letter, to force its terminology, the immediate *donné* of the sentence, to accept certain substitutions, certain simplifications; we must now return to the most superficial level; for the maxim's structure, however formal, is itself dressed out in a subtle and sparkling form, which constitutes its luster and its pleasure (there is a pleasure of maxims); this hard and brilliant garment is what we call *point.* When I read: "It is a kind of coquetry to make others notice that one never indulges in it," I sense an aesthetic intention on the level of the sentence; I see that it consists in making the word *coquetry* serve two different projects, unhooking, so to speak, one from the other, so that not indulging in coquetry becomes a coquetry in its turn; in short, I am dealing with a veritable verbal construction: this is point (which we also find in verse). What is point? It is, if you like, the maxim constituted as a spectacle; like every spectacle, this one intends a pleasure (inherited from a whole *précieux* tradition, whose history no longer needs to be written); but what is most interesting is that like every spectacle, too, but with infinitely more ingenuity (since we are concerned here with language and not with space), point is a form of rupture: it always tends to *close* thought on a flourish, on that fragile moment when the word is stilled, touching on both silence and applause.

Point is, in fact, almost always at the maxim's end. Frequently, even, like every good artist, La Rochefoucauld prepares us for it—without our suspecting as much; the maxim begins within ordinary discourse (this is not yet a maxim); then it gathers toward its point, explodes and closes its truth. This passage of discourse to point is usually signaled by a humble conjunction: *and;* this *and* adds nothing, contrary to its habitual function; it *opens,* it is the curtain which parts and discovers the stage of words: "Happiness is in our taste, not in things; and it is by loving what we love that we love, not by loving what others find lovable": the entire ending, with its antithesis and its inverted identity, is a kind of suddenly revealed spectacle. For of course it is antithesis which is the preferred figure of point; it seizes upon all grammatical categories, substantives (for instance, *ruin/establishment, reason/nature, humor/wit,* etc.), adjectives *(large/small),* and the apparently humblest pronouns *(one/the other),* once they are set in significative opposition; and beyond grammar, it can invade movements, themes, can oppose, for example, all expressions of *above* (to rise) to all those of *below* (to sink). In the world of the maxim, antithesis is a universal power of signification, to the point where it can make spectacular (or pertinent, as the linguists would say) a simple contrast of numbers; this one, for instance: "There is only one kind of love, but it has a thousand different copies," in which it is the opposition *one/a thousand* which constitutes point. Whereby we see that antithesis is not only an emphatic figure, i.e., no more than a simple decor of thought; it is probably something else and something more; a way of producing meaning from an opposition of terms; and as we know from recent explorations of linguistics that this is the fundamental procedure of signification (and even, according to some physiologists, of perception), we are in a better position to realize how antithesis functions so well in such archaic languages as verse and aphorism; antithesis is ultimately no more than a mechanism quite devoid of meaning, and since, in every developed society, the return to origins ultimately functions as a surprising spectacle, antithesis has thus become a kind of *point*, which is to say, the very spectacle of meaning

To alternate, then, is one of the two procedures of point. The other, which is often complementary to it, though opposed, is *to repeat*. Conventional rhetoric used to proscribe (and still does) repetitions of the same word too close together; Pascal had derided this formal law, insisting that we not forget meaning on some harmonious pretext: there are cases when we must call Paris Paris, and others when we must call it the capital of France: it is meaning which rules repetition. The maxim, however, goes further: it likes to repeat a term, especially if this repetition can mark an antithesis: "We weep to avoid the shame of not weeping;" such repetition can be fragmentary, which permits repeating a part of the word without repeating the word itself: "Interest speaks all kinds of languages, and plays all kinds of parts, even that of the disinterested man;" returning here to the linguists' explanation, we may say that the opposition of meaning is all the more flagrant in that it is sustained by a perfectly limited verbal accident: it is only the prefix which opposes *interest* to *disinterested man*. Point is doubtless a game, but this game is in the service of a very old technique, that of meaning; so that writing well is playing with words because playing with words is inevitably coming closer to that intention of opposition which governs the birth of a signification. As we see clearly in certain complex constructions, in which the repetitions extend and interlock so stubbornly that what we might call the oppositional seam becomes spectacularly apparent: meaning bursts out of a sheet of insignificances, as in the case of this maxim: "Philosophy triumphs readily over past evils and evils to come, but present evils triumph over it:" here a sudden dissymmetry disturbs and consequently makes the entire series of surrounding symmetries signify.[1]

Once the forms are posited, we may now approach the contents. It is to the restrictive relation of identity (. . . *is only* . . .), whose demystifying effect has been indicated, that we must return, for whatever its syntactical variations, it is in this relation that the verbal structure of the maxim and the mental structure of its author meet. It unites the strong terms. But from the point of view of meaning, what are these strong terms? The first term, the one which comes at the head of the maxim, precisely the one we are concerned to puncture, is occupied by what we might call the class of *virtues (clemency, valor, strength of soul, sincerity, scorn of death);* these virtues are, so to speak, *irrealia,* vain objects, appearances whose reality must be rediscovered; and this reality is evidently afforded by the second term, the one which has the responsibility of revealing the true identity of the virtues; this second term is therefore occupied by what we might call the class of *realia,* real objects which compose the world of which the virtues are no more than dreams. What are these *realia* which constitute man? They can be of three kinds: first and foremost, there are *passions (vanity, rage, sloth, ambition,* subject to the greatest of all, *self-love);* then there are *contingencies:* which means everything that depends on chance (and for La Rochefoucauld, accident is one of the greatest masters of the world): the accident of events, of occasion, what classical language calls *fortune,* hazard of the body, of physical subjectivity, which this same

---

[1] As we realize by simply casting the maxim as an equation. Let a = *philosophy,* b = *triumph over,* c = *evils* (1, 2, 3 = past, present, and to come). We then get the following false symmetry: a b c$^{1.3}$/c^2 b a.

language calls *humor;* lastly, there is a final class of realities
defined by their interchangeable character; they occasionally
replace the passions or the contingencies, in a more indefinite
fashion; these are certain attenuated realities, expression of a
certain insignificance of the world; these are *actions, flaws,
effects,* general, unemphatic words, ordinarily followed by a
relative pronoun which coins their meaning but also banalizes
it: ". . . an assemblage of actions and interests which fortune
or our own industry manages to arrange;" and since these
words take the place of a term (though without filling it with
a true meaning), we may recognize in them certain *mana words,*
strong by the place they occupy in the structure of the maxim
but devoid—or nearly so—of meaning.[1]

Between *irrealia* (virtues) and *realia* (passions, contingencies, actions), there is a mask relation; the former disguise the
latter; we know that the mask is a great classical theme (in
those days, language spoke not of *masks* but of *veils* or of
paint); the whole second half of the seventeenth century was
riddled by the ambiguity of signs. How to read man? Racinian
tragedy is filled with this uncertainty: faces and actions are
equivocal signals, and this duplicity makes the world *(the
worldly)* overwhelming, to the point where to renounce the
world is to withdraw from the intolerable inexactitude of the
human code. La Rochefoucauld brings this ambiguity of signs
to a halt by unmasking the virtues; no doubt, first of all and
most frequently, the so-called pagan virtues (for example, the
scorn of death), pitilessly reduced to self-love or to unaware-
ness (this reduction was an Augustinian, a Jansenist theme);
but ultimately *all* the virtues; for what matters is to pacify,
even at the price of a pessimistic vision, the unendurable duplicity of *what is seen;* now, to leave an appearance without its

---

[1]For the definition of *mana* to which I am alluding, I refer the reader to
Lévi-Strauss's *Introduction to the Work of Marcel Mauss.*

reductive explanation is to leave a doubt unresolved; for La Rochefoucauld, definition, however bleak, certainly has a restorative function; to show that the moral order is merely the mask of a contingent disorder is ultimately more reassuring than to abide by an apparent but singular order; pessimistic in its result, La Rochefoucauld's procedure is beneficent in its method; it brings to an end, with each maxim, the anxiety of a suspect sign.

Here, then, is a universe which can be organized only in its verticality. On the level of the virtues alone, i.e., of appearances, no structure is possible, since structure derives precisely from a relation of truth between the manifest and the hidden. It follows that the virtues, taken separately, cannot constitute the object of any description; we cannot coordinate heroism, kindness, honesty, and gratitude, for instance, in order to make them into a sheaf of merits, even if we propose to demystify, subsequently, the Good in general; each virtue exists only from the moment we identify what it hides; La Rochefoucauldian man, therefore, cannot be described except in zigzags, according to a sinusoid which runs from the apparent good to the concealed reality. Doubtless there are more important virtues, which is to say, for La Rochefoucauld, more obsessive: but these are precisely the ones where illusion, which is merely the distance from the surface to the depths, is greatest: gratitude, for example, which we might almost see as a neurotic obsession of Jansenist thought, constantly overwhelmed by the intimidation of fidelity (as we see clearly in Racine, where erotic fidelity is always a funereal value), and in a more general way, all the attitudes of good conscience, generalized under the name of *merit:* already an entirely "modern" proposition, merit is ultimately, for La Rochefoucauld, no more than bad faith.

Hence there is no possible system of the virtues, if we do not descend to the realities of which they are merely the reversal.

The paradoxical result of this dialectic is finally the real disorder of man (disorder of the passions, of events, of the humors), which gives this man his unity. We cannot establish a structure of the virtues, for they are merely parasitical values; but we can much more readily assign an order to the disorder of *realia*. What order? not that of an organization, but that of a force, or better still of an *energy*. Passion and fortune are active principles, disorder *creates* the world: the disorder of contingencies causes, for better or worse, the only life which is granted us. Confronted with the passions and accidents of life, La Rochefoucauld shows a certain eloquence, he speaks of them almost as though they were persons; these forces organize themselves into a hierarchy; ruling them all, self-love. This self-love has virtually the properties of a chemical, one might almost say a magical, substance—since this substance is at once vital and unitary; it can be infinitesimal (as indicated by the adjectives *subtle, fine, hidden, delicate*), without losing any of its power, quite the contrary; it is everywhere, deep within the virtues, of course, but also deep within the other passions, such as jealousy or ambition, which are merely their varieties: it transmutes everything, the virtues into passions, but also sometimes, so unlimited is its power, the passions into virtues, egoism for instance into kindness; it is a Proteus; as a power of disorder, passion (or self-love, it comes to the same thing) is an active, a tormenting god; by its incessant action, at once multiform and monotonous, it brings into the world an obsession, a ground bass whose profusion of various behaviors is merely its counterpoint: the repeated disorder is ultimately an order, the only one which is granted us. Now, by dint of constituting passion as an active principle, La Rochefoucauld was obliged to bring an acute, subtle, anxious, astonished attention to bear on man's inertias, to those kinds of toneless passions which are in a sense the negative, or better still, the *scandal* of passion: *weakness* and *sloth*; there are several penetrating maxims on this subject; how can man be both inactive and impassioned? La Rochefoucauld had the intuition of that dialectic which makes negativity into a force; he understood that there is a resistance to passion in man, but that this resistance was not a virtue, a voluntary effort toward the good, but that, on the contrary, it was a second passion, more cunning than the first; this is why he regards it with an absolute pessimism; the active passions are finally more estimable, because they have a form; sloth (or weakness) is more inimical to virtue than vice is: it nourishes hypocrisy, operates on the frontier of the virtues, for instance, it assumes the mask of gentleness; it is the one defect which man cannot correct in himself. His fundamental flaw is precisely, by his sluggishness, to prevent the very dialectic of good and evil: for example, we cannot be good without a certain meanness; but when man lets himself be overtaken by the sloth of meanness, it is goodness itself which is ineluctibly taken from him.

As we see, there is in this *profound* structure a certain vertigo of nothingness; descending from level to level, from heroism to ambition, from ambition to jealousy, we never touch bottom, we can never give an ultimate definition of man which might be irreducible; when the ultimate passion has been designated, this passion itself vanishes away, it can be nothing but sloth, inertia, nothingness; the maxim is an endless trail of demystification; man is no more than a skeleton of passions, and this skeleton itself is perhaps no more than the hallucination of a nothing: *man is not certain.* This vertigo of the unreal is perhaps the ransom of all enterprises of demystification, so that what corresponds to the greatest lucidity is often the greatest unreality. Once we begin ridding man of his masks, how and where to stop? The way is all the more surely barred for La Rochefoucauld in that the philosophy of his time afforded him only a world composed of essences; the only relation which one could reasonably impute to these essences was a relation of identity, which is to say a motionless relation, closed to the dialectical ideas of return, of circularity, of process or transitivity; it is not that La Rochefoucauld did not have a certain imagination of what was then called *contrariety;* on this point, some of his maxims are strangely modern; granted the separation of moral or passional essences, he saw clearly that they could perform certain exchanges, that evil could emerge from good, that an excess could change the quality of a thing; the very object of his "pessimism" is, in the long run, at the end of the maxim, outside the maxim, the world, the actions which one can or cannot perform there, in short, the order of *praxis,* as we might say today; this presentiment of a transformation of fatal essences by human *praxis* we see clearly in the frequent distinction La Rochefoucauld establishes between the substance of an action *(to love, to praise)* and its mode of performance or fulfillment: "We sometimes believe we hate flattery, but we hate only the mode of flattering;" or again: "Agreeable as it is, love pleases still more by the ways in which it shows itself than by itself." But at the very moment when La Rochefoucauld seems to affirm the world by recuperating the dialectic in this way, an evidently moral project intervenes, which immobilizes the lifelike description under the terrorist definition, the observation under the ambiguities of a law, which is given both as morality and as physis. Now, this impotence to arrest the demystification of the world at a certain moment is in the very form of the *Maxims,* in that restrictive relation of identity to which we must therefore return once more. For if the virtues occupy the first term of the relation, and the passions, contingencies, and actions the second term, and if the second term demystifies the first, this means that the appearance (or the mask) constitutes the subject of the discourse and that reality is merely its predicate; in other words, the whole world is seen, *centered,* one might say in photographic terms, in the guise of seeming,

whose being is nothing more than an attribute; of course La
Rochefoucauld's procedure seems objective at first glance,
since it seeks to rediscover being beneath appearances, the
reality of passions under the alibi of noble feelings; but this
authentic project of truth remains so to speak immobilized,
spellbound in the form of the maxim: no matter how much La
Rochefoucauld denounces the great entities of moral life as
pure dreams, he nonetheless constitutes these dreams as *subjects* of discourse, of which, finally, all consequent *explanation*
remains a prisoner: the virtues are dreams, but petrified
dreams: these masks occupy the entire stage; we exhaust ourselves seeing through them yet without ever quite leaving
them: the *Maxims* are ultimately a nightmare of truth.

The infinite demystification which the *Maxims* stage for us
could not fail to involve (to expose) the maxim-maker himself:
there are maxims on maxims; this one, for example:

> We have as many reasons to complain of those who teach us
> to know ourselves as had the Athenian madman to complain
> of the doctor who cured him of the notion that he was rich.

Here La Rochefoucauld approaches, obliquely and by a period
reference to the moralists of antiquity, the very status of the
demystifier within the group which he simultaneously ex-
presses and attacks. The author of maxims is not a writer; he
tells the truth (at least, that is his declared project), that is his
function: hence he rather prefigures the man whom we call the
intellectual. Now, the intellectual is entirely defined by a contradictory status; certainly he is delegated by his group (here,
worldly society) to a specific task, but this task is to raise
questions; in other words, society charges a man, a *rhetor*, to
turn against itself and to contest it. Such is the ambiguous link
which seems to unite La Rochefoucauld with his caste; the
maxim is a direct product of the salons, as we are informed by

a thousand historical testimonies; and yet the maxim constantly contests worldliness; everything occurs as if worldly society indulged itself, through La Rochefoucauld, in the spectacle of its own contestation; doubtless this contestation is not really dangerous, since it is not political, but only psychological, authorized moreover by the Christian climate; how could this disabused aristocracy have turned against its own activity, since this activity was not work but leisure? La Rochefoucauld's contestation, at once harsh and inadequate, defines quite nicely the limits which a caste must assign to its own interrogation if it wants that interrogation to be both purifying and innocuous: the very limits of what will for three centuries be called *psychology*.

In short, the group asks the intellectual to discern in himself the—contradictory—reasons for contesting it and for representing it, and perhaps it is this tension, livelier here than elsewhere, which gives La Rochefoucauld's *Maxims* a disconcerting character, at least if we judge them from our modern point of view; the work, in its discontinuity, ceaselessly alternates between the greatest originality and the greatest banality; here, maxims whose intelligence and, in fact, whose modernity astonish and exalt us; there, platitudes and truisms (which does not mean they are true), all the more colorless in that a whole literature has subsequently banalized them *ad nauseam;* the maxim is a two-faced being, here tragic, there bourgeois; despite its austere stamp, its stinging and pure writing, it is essentially an ambiguous discourse, located on the frontier of two worlds. Which ones? We can say, that of death and that of play. On death's side, we have the tragic question *par excellence,* addressed by man to the silent god: *Who am I?* This is the question ceaselessly formulated by the Racinian hero, Eriphyle, for instance, who keeps trying to know herself and who dies of the effort; this is also the question of the *Maxims:* it is answered by the terrible, the funereal *is only* of restrictive identity, and again, as we have seen, this answer itself is uncertain, since man never definitively abandons the dream of virtue. But this mortal question is also, *par excellence,* the question of every form of play. Interrogating Oedipus as to the nature of man, the Sphinx established both tragic discourse and ludic discourse, the game of death (since for Oedipus the wages of ignorance was death) and the game of the salon. *Who are you?* This riddle is also the question of the *Maxims;* as we have seen, everything, in their structure, is very close to a verbal game, not, of course, to a chance conflagration of words as the surrealists might conceive it—they too, moreover, great maxim-makers—but at least to a submission of meaning to certain pre-established forms, as if the formal rule were an instrument of truth. We know that La Rochefoucauld's maxims are, in fact, a product of salon games (portraits, riddles, sentences); and this encounter of the tragic and the worldly, one grazing the other, is not the least of the truths which the *Maxims* propose for us: their discoveries may here and there pass, swept away by men's history, but their project remains, which says that the game touches on the death of the subject.

(1961)

The Plates
of
the Encyclopedia

Our literature has taken a long time to discover the object; we must wait till Balzac for the novel to be the space not only of pure human relations but also of substances and usages called upon to play their part in the story of passions: could Grandet have been a miser (literarily speaking) without his candle ends, his lumps of sugar, and his gold crucifix? Long before literature, the *Encyclopedia*, particularly in its plates, practices what we might call a certain philosophy of the object, i.e., reflects on its being, produces at once an inventory and a definition; technological purpose no doubt compelled the description of objects; but by separating image from text, the *Encyclopedia* committed itself to an autonomous iconography of the object whose power we enjoy today, since we no longer look at these illustrations with mere information in mind.

The plates of the *Encyclopedia* present the object, and this presentation already adds to the illustration's didactic purpose a more gratuitous justification, of an aesthetic or oneiric order: the imagery of the *Encyclopedia* can best be compared with one of those Great Expositions held the world over in the last century or so, and of which, in its period, the Encyclopedic illustration was a kind of ancestor: in both cases, we are concerned with a census and a spectacle: we consult the plates of the *Encyclopedia* as we would visit today's World's Fair in Brussels or New York. The objects presented are literally encyclopedic, i.e., they cover the entire sphere of substances shaped by man: clothes, vehicles, tools, weapons, instruments, furniture, all that man makes out of wood, metal, glass, or fiber is catalogued here, from the chisel to the statue, from the artificial flower to the ship. This Encyclopedic object is ordinarily apprehended by the image on three levels: anthological, since the object, isolated from any context, is presented *in itself;* anecdotic, when it is "naturalized" by its insertion into a large-scale *tableau vivant* (which is what we call a vignette); genetic, when the image offers us the trajectory from raw substance to finished object: genesis, essence, praxis, the object is thus accounted for in all its categories: sometimes it *is,* sometimes it is *made,* sometimes it even *makes.* Of these three states, assigned here and there to the object-as-image, one is certainly favored by the *Encyclopedia:* that of birth: it is good to be able to show how we can produce things from their very nonexistence and thus to credit man with an extraordinary power of creation: here is a countryside; the plenitude of nature (meadows, hills, trees) constitutes a kind of human void from which we cannot see what will emerge; yet the image moves, objects are born, precursors of humanity: lines are drawn on the earth, stakes are pounded in, holes dug; a cross-section shows us, beneath a desert nature, the powerful network of galleries and lodes: a mine is born. This is a kind of symbol: Encyclopedic man *mines* all nature with human signs; in the Encyclopedic landscape, we are never alone; however strong the elements, there is always a fraternal *product* of man: the object is the world's human signature.

We know that a simple substance can make a whole story legible: Brecht has rediscovered the wretched essence of the

Thirty Years' War by the radical treatment of fabrics, wicker, and wood. The Encyclopedic object emerges from general substances which are still those of the artisanal era. If we visit a World's Fair today, we perceive in all the objects exhibited two or three dominant substances, glass, metal, plastic no doubt; the substance of the Encyclopedic object is of a more vegetal age: it is wood which dominates in this great catalogue; it produces a world of objects easy on the eyes, already human by their substance, resistant but not brittle, constructible but not plastic. Nothing shows wood's humanizing power better than the *Encyclopedia*'s machines; in this world of technology (which is still artisanal, for the industrial is as yet unborn), the machine is obviously a capital object; now most of the *Encyclopedia*'s machines are made out of wood; they are enormous, highly complicated scaffoldings in which metal frequently supplies only notched wheels. The wood which constitutes them keeps them subservient to a certain notion of *play:* these machines are (for us) like big toys; contrary to modern images, man, always present in some corner of the machine, does not accompany it in a simple relation of surveillance; turning a crank, pressing a pedal, spinning a thread, he participates in the machine in a manner that is both active and delicate; the engraver represents him for the most part dressed neatly as a gentleman; this is not a worker but a little lord who plays on a kind of technological organ, all of whose gears and wheels are exposed; what is striking about the Encyclopedic machine is its absence of secrecy; in it there is no hidden place (spring or housing) which would magically conceal energy, as is the case with our modern machines (it is the myth of electricity to be a self-generated, hence enclosed, power); the energy here is essentially transmission, amplification of a simple human movement; the Encyclopedic machine is never anything but an enormous relay; man is at one term, the object at the other; between the two, an architectural milieu, consisting of beams, ropes, and gears, through which, like a light, human strength is simultaneously developed, refined, focused, and enlarged: hence, in the gauze-loom, a little man in a jacket, sitting at the keyboard of a huge wooden machine, produces an extremely fine web, as if he were playing music; elsewhere, in a completely bare room, containing only a maze of wood and tarred ropes, a young women sitting on a bench turns a crank, while her other hand rests gently on her knee. A *simpler* idea of technology is inconceivable.

An almost naïve simplicity, a kind of Golden Legend of artisanry (for there is no trace of social distress): the *Encyclopedia* identifies the simple, the elementary, the essential, and the causal. Encyclopedic technology is simple because it is reduced to a two-term space: the causal trajectory which proceeds from substance to object; hence all the plates which involve some technological operation (of transformation) mobilize an aesthetic of bareness: huge, empty, well-lighted rooms, in which man cohabits alone with his work: a space without parasites, walls bare, tables cleared; the simple, here, is nothing but the vital; this is made explicit in the bakery; as a primary element, bread implies an austere site; on the other hand, pastry, belonging to the order of the superfluous, proliferates in instruments, operations, products, whose fussy ensemble constitutes a certain *baroque.* In a general way, the object's *production* sweeps the image toward an almost sacred simplicity; its *use,* on the other hand (represented at the moment of sale, in the shop), authorizes an embellishment of the vignette, abounding in instruments, accessories, and attitudes: austerity of creation, luxury of commerce, such is the double regime of the Encyclopedic object: the density of the image and its ornamental charge always signifies that we are shifting from production to consumption.

Of course, the object's pre-eminence in this world derives from an inventorying effort, but inventory is never a neutral idea; to catalogue is not merely to ascertain, as it appears at first glance, but also to appropriate. The *Encyclopedia* is a huge ledger of ownership; Bernard Groetheuysen has noted an opposition between the *orbis pictus* of the Renaissance, animated by the spirit of an adventurous knowledge, and the encyclopedism of the eighteenth century, based on a learning of appropriation. Formally (this is apparent in the plates), ownership depends on a certain dividing up of things: to appropriate is to fragment the world, to divide it into finite objects subject to man in proportion to their very discontinuity: for we cannot separate without finally naming and classifying, and at that moment, property is born. In mythic terms, possession of the world began not with Genesis but at the Flood, when man was obliged to name each kind of animal and to house it, i.e., to separate it from its next of species; the *Encyclopedia,* moreover, takes an essentially pragmatic view of Noah's ark; for it, the ark is not a ship—an object always more or less *oneiric*— but a long floating crate, a goods locker; the only problem it appears to offer the *Encyclopedia* is certainly not theological: it is the problem of its construction, or even, in more technical terms, as is only right, of its framing, and even more specifically, of its fenestration, since each of its windows corresponds to a typical pair of animals, thus divided, named, domesticated (docilely sticking their heads out the opening).

Encyclopedic nomenclature, whatever its technological esotericism on occasion, actually establishes a familiar possession. This is remarkable, for nothing logically obliges the object to be invariably friendly to man. The object, quite the contrary, is humanly a very ambiguous thing; we have noted that for a long time our literature did not acknowledge it; later (which is to say, on the whole, today), the object has been endowed with an unfortunate opacity; assimilated to an inhuman state of nature, its proliferation cannot be noted without a sentiment of apocalypse or of alienation: the modern object

is either asphyxiation (Ionesco) or nausea (Sartre). The Encyclopedic object is on the contrary subjugated (we might say
that it is precisely pure *object* in the etymological sense of the
term), for a very simple and constant reason: it is on each
occasion *signed* by man; the image is the privileged means of
this human presence, for it permits discreetly locating a per-
manent man on the object's horizon; the plates of the *Encyclopedia* are always populated (they afford thereby a close relationship with another "progressive" or, to be more precise,
bourgeois iconography: seventeenth-century Dutch painting);
you can imagine the most naturally solitary, "savage" object;
be sure that man will nonetheless appear in a corner of the
image; he will be considering the object, or measuring it, or
surveying it, using it at least as a spectacle; take the Giant's
Causeway, that mass of terrifying basalt composed by nature
at Antrim, in Ireland; this inhuman landscape is, one might
say, stuffed with humanity; gentlemen in tricornes, lovely la-
dies contemplate the horrible landscape, chatting familiarly;
farther on, men are fishing, scientists are weighing the mineral
substance: analyzed into functions (spectacle, fishing, science),
the basalt is *reduced,* tamed, familiarized, because it is *divided:*
what is striking in the entire *Encyclopedia* (and especially in its
images) is that it proposes a *world without fear* (we shall see in
a moment that the monstrous is not excluded, but in a category
much more "surrealist" than terrifying). We can even specify
more clearly what the man of the Encyclopedic image is reduced to—what is, in some sense, the very essence of his humanity: his hands. In many plates (and not the least beautiful),
hands, severed from any body, flutter around the work (for
their lightness is extreme); these hands are doubtless the symbol of an artisanal world (again we are concerned with traditional, virtually unmechanized trades, the steam engine is kept
out of sight), as is seen by the importance of the tables (huge,
flat, well lighted, often encircled by hands); but beyond arti-

sanship, the hands are inevitably the inductive sign of the human essence: do we not see even today, in a less obvious fashion, that our advertising constantly returns to this mysterious motif, at once natural and supernatural, as if man could not get over having hands? It is not easy to be done with a civilization of the hand.

Hence in the immediate state of its representations, the *Encyclopedia* is constantly concerned to familiarize the world of objects (which is its primary substance) by adding to it the obsessive cipher of man. Yet beyond the letter of the image, this humanization implies an intellectual system of an extreme subtlety: the Encyclopedic image is human not only because man is represented in it but also because it constitutes a structure of *information*. This structure, though iconographic, is articulated in most instances like real language (the one which, in fact, we call *articulate*), whose two dimensions as revealed by structural linguistics it reproduces: we know, in fact, that all discourse involves signifying units and that these units are ordered according to two axes, one of substitution (paradigmatic), the other of contiguity (syntagmatic); each unit can thereby *vary* (potentially) with its parents, and *link* (in reality) with its neighbors. This is what happens, *grosso modo,* in an *Encyclopedia* plate. The majority of these plates are formed of two parts; in the lower part, the tool or the gesture (the object of the demonstration), isolated from any real context, is shown in its essence; it constitutes the informative unit, and this unit is generally *varied:* its aspects, elements, kinds are detailed; this part of the plate has the role of *declining* the object, of manifesting its paradigm; on the contrary, in the upper part or vignette, this same object (and its varieties) is apprehended in a lively scene (generally a scene of sale or manufacture, shop or workroom), linked to other objects within a real situation: here we rediscover the syntagmatic dimension of the message; and just as in oral discourse the system of the language, perceptible chiefly on the paradigmatic level, is somehow *hidden* behind the living stream of words, in the same way the Encyclopedic plate plays simultaneously on intellectual demonstration (by its objects) and on fictive life (by its scenes). Here is a trade plate (the pastrycook): down below, the ensemble of various instruments necessary to the profession; in this paradigmatic state, the instrument has no life: inert, frozen in its essence, it is merely a demonstrative schema, analogous to the quasi-academic form of a verbal or nominal paradigm; up above, on the contrary, the chopping board, the whisk (the pastrycooks were making *pâtés en croûte*), the sieve, the molds are arranged, linked together, "enacted" in a *tableau vivant,* exactly as the "cases" distinguished by grammar are ordinarily given without our thinking of them in real discourse, with this difference, that the Encyclopedic syntagm is of an extreme density of meaning; in informational language, we would say that the scene involves little "noise" (see, for instance, the workshop in which the chief operations of engraving are gathered together).

Most of the objects from the lower paradigm are therefore reassembled in the vignette under the heading of signs; whereas the figured nomenclature of the instruments, utensils, products, and gestures involves by definition no secrecy, the vignette, charged with a disseminated meaning, always presents itself a little like a riddle: we must decipher it, locate in it the informative units. The vignette has the riddle's actual density: *all* the information must turn up in the experienced scene (whence, upon scrutiny, a certain exploration of meaning); in the plate devoted to cotton, a certain number of accidents must necessarily refer to the exoticism of the vegetal realm: the palm, the stubble, the island, the Chinaman's shaved head, his long pipe (impractical, it would seem, for working with cotton but which evokes the image of opium), none of this information is innocent: the image is crammed with demonstrative significations; analogously, Demosthenes' lantern is admirable *because* two men are discussing it and pointing to it; it is an antiquity *because* it adjoins a ruin; it is situated in Greece *because* there is the sea, a boat; we contemplate its present state *because* a band of men are dancing in a ring nearby, performing something like the *bouzouki.* Of this kind of cryptographic vocation of the image, there is no better symbol than the two plates dedicated to the hemispheres; a sphere, enclosed by a fine network of lines, makes legible the outline of its continents; but these lines and these contours are only a light transparency behind which float, like a meaning *from behind,* the figures of the constellations (the Wagoner, the Dolphin, the Scales, the Dog).

However, the vignette, a condensate of meaning, also offers a resistance to meaning, and we might say that it is in this resistance, paradoxically, that the plate's language becomes a complete, an adult language. It is, as a matter of fact, apparent that for a reader of the period the scene itself often involves very little new information: who had not seen a pastrycook's shop, a tilled field, a river fishery? The vignette's function is therefore elsewhere: the syntagm (since it is with it that we are concerned) tells us here, once again, that language (and *a fortiori,* iconic language) is not pure intellectual communication: meaning is completed only when it is somehow naturalized in a complete action of man; for the *Encyclopedia,* too, there is a message only *in situation,* whereby we see how ambiguous, finally, the *Encyclopedia's* didacticism is: very strong in the lower (paradigmatic) part of the plate, it is diluted at its syntagmatic level, to join (without actually being lost) what we must, in fact, call the fictive truth of any human action. At its demonstrative stage, the Encyclopedic plate constitutes a *radical language,* consisting of pure concepts, with neither word tools nor syntax; at the higher stage, this radical language becomes a human *langue,* it deliberately loses in intelligibility what it gains in experience.

The vignette does not have only an existential function, but also, one might say, an *epic* one; it is entrusted to represent the glorious term of a great trajectory, that of substance, transformed, sublimated by man, through a series of episodes and stations: this is symbolized perfectly by the cross-section of the mill, where we see the grain proceed from story to story to be resolved into flour. The demonstration becomes even stronger when it is deliberately artificial: through the weapon shop's open door, we see two men dueling out in the street: the scene is unlikely, though logical if one wants to show the ultimate term of the operation (subject of the plate), which is small-arms supply: there is a trajectory of the object which must be honored to the end. This trajectory is often paradoxical (whence the interest in showing the terms clearly); an enormous mass of wood and cordage produces a delicate flowered carpet: the finished object, so different from the apparatus which has given birth to it, is placed in view; the effect and the cause, juxtaposed, form a figure of meaning by contiguity (what is called metonymy): the framing of the loom finally *signifies* the carpet. The paradox reaches its (delicious) apogee when we can no longer perceive any relation of substance between the initial substance and the object arrived at: at the card-maker's, the playing cards are generated out of a void, the hole in the cardboard; in the workshop of the artificial-flower maker, not only does nothing recall the flower, but even the operations which lead to it are constantly antipathetic to the idea of the flower: these are stampings, stencilings, hammer taps, punch-outs: what relation between such shows of strength and the anemone's fragile efflorescence? Precisely a human relation, the relation of the omnipotent praxis of man, which out of nothing can make everything.

Thus the *Encyclopedia* constantly testifies to a certain epic of substance, but this epic is also in a sense that of the mind: the trajectory of substance is nothing, for the Encyclopedist, but the progress of reason: the image has a logical function *as well*.

Diderot says as much explicitly apropos of the machine for making stockings, whose image will reproduce structure: *"We may regard it as a single and unique reasoning of which the work's fabrication is the conclusion; therefore there reigns among its parts so great a dependence that were we to remove even a single one, or to alter the form of those regarded as least important, we should destroy the entire mechanism."* Here we find prophetically formulated the very principle of cybernetic ensembles; the plate, image of the machine, is indeed in its way a brain; we introduce substance into it and set up the "program": the vignette (the syntagm) serves as a conclusion. This logical character of the image has another model, that of dialectics: the image analyzes, first enumerating the scattered elements of the object or of the operation and flinging them as on a table before the reader's eyes, then recomposing them, even adding to them the density of the scene, i.e., of life. The Encyclopedic mounting is based on reason: it descends into analysis as deeply as is necessary in order to *"perceive the elements without confusion"* (according to another phrase of Diderot's, precisely apropos of the drawings, results of investigations on the spot made by draughtsmen in the workshops): the image is a kind of rational synopsis: it illustrates not only the object or its trajectory but also the very mind which conceives it; this double movement corresponds to a double reading; if you read the plate from bottom to top, you obtain in a sense an experiential reading, you relive the object's epic trajectory, its flowering in the complex world of consumers; you proceed from nature to sociality; but if you read the image from top to bottom, starting from the vignette, it is the progress of the analytic mind that you are reproducing; the world gives you the usual, the evident (the scene); with the Encyclopedist, you descend gradually to causes, to substances, to primary elements, you proceed from the experiential to the causal, you intellectualize the object. The privilege of the image—opposed in this to writing, which is linear—is to compel our reading to have no specific meaning: an image is always deprived of a logical vector (as certain modern experiences tend to prove); those of the *Encyclopedia* possess a precious circularity: we can read them starting from the experiential or, on the contrary, from the intelligible: the real world is not reduced, it is suspended between two great orders of reality, in truth, irreducible orders.

Such is the informative system of the Encyclopedic image. Yet the information does not end with what the image could say to the reader of its period: the modern reader also receives from this old image certain information which the Encyclopedist could not foresee: historical information, first of all: it is quite evident that the plates of the *Encyclopedia* are a mine of precious data as to the civilization of the eighteenth century (at least of its first half); oneiric information, if one may put it so, subsequently: the period object stirs in us certain strictly modern analogies; here is a phenomenon of connotation (connotation, a specific linguistic notion, is constituted by the development of a second meaning) which profoundly justifies the new edition of the old documents. Take, for example, the Lyons diligence; the *Encyclopedia* could aim at nothing but the objective—matte, one might say—reproduction of a certain means of transport; now it happens that this massive and closed trunk immediately wakens in us what we might call memories of the imagination: stories of bandits, kidnappings, ransoms, nocturnal transfers of mysterious prisoners, and, even closer to us, Westerns, the whole heroic and sinister myth of the mail coach is there, in this black object, innocently given, as a photograph of the period might have given it to us. There is a *depth* in the Encyclopedic image, the very depth of time which transforms the object into myth.

This leads to what we must call the Poetics of the Encyclopedic image, if we agree to define Poetics as the sphere of the infinite vibrations of meaning, at the center of which is placed the literal object. We can say that there is not one plate of the *Encyclopedia* which fails to vibrate well beyond its demonstrative intent. This singular vibration is above all an astonishment. Of course, the Encyclopedic image is always clear; but in a deeper region of ourselves, beyond the intellect, or at least in its profile, certain questions are born and exceed us. Consider the astonishing image of man reduced to his network of veins; here anatomical boldness unites with the great poetic and philosophic interrogation: *What is it?* What name to give it? How give a name? A thousand names rise up, dislodging each other: a tree, a bear, a monster, a hair shirt, a .fabric, everything which overflows the human silhouette, distends it, draws it toward regions remote from itself, makes it overstep the divisions of nature; yet, just as in the sketch of a master, the swarm of pencil strokes finally resolves into a pure and exact form, perfectly signifying, so here all the vibrations of meaning concur to impose upon us a certain idea of the object; in this initially human, then animal, then vegetal form we still recognize a kind of unique matter—vein, hair, or thread—and we accede to that great undifferentiated substance of which verbal or pictural poetry is the mode of knowledge: confronting the man of the *Encyclopedia* we must say *the fibrous,* as the ancient Greeks said *the moist* or *the warm* or *the round:* a certain essence of substance is here affirmed.

As a matter of fact, there cannot be anarchic poetry. The iconography of the *Encyclopedia* is poetic because its overflows of meaning always have a certain unity, suggest an ultimate meaning transcending all the *essays* of meaning. For example: the image of the womb is actually quite enigmatic; yet its metaphoric vibrations (as if it were a flayed ox, the interior of a body which dissolves and floats away) do not contradict the original traumatism attached to this object. There is a certain horror and a certain fascination common to some objects, which precisely establishes them in a homogeneous *class,* whose unity and identity is affirmed by Poetics. It is this profound order of metaphor which justifies—poetically—the recourse to a certain category of the *monstrous* (at least, according to the law of connotation, this is what we perceive in the presence of certain plates): anatomical monsters, as in the case of the enigmatic womb or that of the bust with the arms cut off, the breast opened, the face thrown back (meant to show the arteries of the thorax); surrealist monsters (those equestrian statues sheathed in wax and cords), huge and incomprehensible objects (halfway between the stocking and the wallet and which are neither one nor the other, in the stocking loom), subtler monsters (plates of poison with sharp, black crystals); all these transgressions of nature make us understand that the poetic (for the monstrous can only be the poetic) is never established except by a displacement of the level of perception: it is one of the *Encyclopedia*'s great gifts to *vary* (in the musical sense of the term) the level on which one and the same object can be perceived, thereby liberating the very secrets of form: seen through the microscope, the flea becomes a horrible monster, caparisoned with plates of bronze, armed with steel spines, with the head of a wicked bird, and this monster achieves the strange sublimity of mythological dragons; elsewhere, and in another key, the snowflake, enlarged, becomes a complicated and harmonious flower. Is poetry not a certain power of *disproportion,* as Baudelaire saw so well, describing the effects of reduction and focusing that hashish induces?

Another exemplary category of the poetic (alongside the monstrous): a certain *immobility.* We always praise the movement of a drawing. Yet, by an inevitable paradox, the *image* of movement can only be arrested; in order to signify itself, movement must be immobilized at the extreme point of its course; it is this incredible, untenable repose that Baudelaire called the emphatic truth of gesture and that we find in demonstrative painting—that of Gros, for instance; to this

suspended, oversignifying gesture we might give the name
numen, for it is indeed the gesture of a god who silently creates
man's fate, i.e., meaning. In the *Encyclopedia,* numinous gestures abound, for what man makes cannot be insignificant. In
the chemical laboratory, for example, each character offers us
slightly impossible actions, for in truth an action cannot be
simultaneously effective and significant, a gesture cannot be
altogether an action: the boy washing the pans, oddly, is not
looking at what he is doing; his face, turned toward us, grants
the operation he is performing a kind of demonstrative solitude; and if the two chemists are having a discussion, it is
necessary that one of them raise a finger to signify by this
emphatic gesture the learned character of the conversation.
Similarly, in the drawing academy, the students are *caught* at
the most improbable moment of their agitation. There is, in
fact, a physical order in which Zeno's paradox is true, when
the arrow flies and yet does not, flies by not flying, and this
order is that of painting (here, of drawing).

As we see, Encyclopedic poetics are always defined as a
certain unrealism. It is the *Encyclopedia*'s wager (in its plates)
to be both a didactic work, based consequently on a severe
demand for objectivity (for "reality"), and a poetic work in
which the real is constantly overcome by *some other thing* (the
other is the sign of all mysteries). By purely graphic means,
which never resort to the noble alibi of *art,* Encyclopedic
drawing explodes the exact world it takes as its subject. We
may specify the meaning of this subversion which affects not
only ideology (and in this the *Encyclopedia*'s plates singularly
enlarge the dimensions of the enterprise) but also, in a much
more serious manner, human rationality. In its very order
(described here in the form of the syntagm and the paradigm,
the vignette and the bottom of the page), the Encyclopedic
plate accomplishes this *risk* of reason. The vignette, a realistic
representation of a simple, familiar world (shops, workshops,

landscapes) is linked to a certain tranquil evidence of the
world: the vignette is calm, reassuring; what can be more
deliciously domestic than the kitchen garden with its enclos-
ing walls, its espaliers in the sun? What can be happier, more
docile, than the fisherman at his line, the tailor sitting at his
window, the feather vendors and the child talking to them? In
this Encyclopedic heaven (the upper part of the plates), evil is
infrequent; scarcely a trace of discomfort over the hard labors
of the glassworkers, armed with pathetic tools, poorly pro-
tected against the terrible heat; and when Nature darkens,
there always remains a man somewhere to reassure us: a fisherman with a torch beside the night sea, a scientist discoursing
before the black basalts of Antrim, the surgeon's light hand
resting on the body he is cutting open, figures of knowledge
inserted into the heart of the storm (in the engraving of wa-
terspouts). Yet as soon as we leave the vignette for the more
analytic plates or images, the world's peaceful order gives way
to a certain *violence*. All the forces of reason and unreason
concur in this poetic disquiet; first of all metaphor itself makes
an infinitely ambiguous object out of a simple, literal object:
the sea urchin is *also* a sun, a monstrance: the named world is
never certain, constantly fascinated by divined and inaccessible essences; and then, above all (and this is the final interrogation raised by these plates), the analytic mind itself, armed
with triumphant reason, can only double the explained world
by a new world *to be explained,* according to a process of infinite
circularity which is that of the dictionary itself, wherein the
world can be defined only by other words; by "entering" into
details, by displacing the levels of perception, by revealing the
hidden, by isolating the elements from their practical context,
by giving objects an abstract essence, in short by "opening up"
nature, the Encyclopedic image can only, at a certain moment,
transcend nature, attaining to a supernature: it is by dint of
didacticism that a kind of wild surrealism is generated here (a

phenomenon which we also find in an ambiguous mode in the disturbing encyclopedia Flaubert gives us in *Bouvard and Pécuchet*): do we want to show how equestrian statues are cast? We must wrap them in an extravagant apparatus of wax, tapes, and supports: what madness could attain to this *limit* (not to mention the violent demystification which reduces a warrior Louis XIV to this monstrous doll)? In a general way, the *Encyclopedia* is fascinated, at reason's instance, by the *wrong side* of things: it cross-sections, it amputates, it turns inside out, it tries to get *behind* nature. Now any "wrong side" is disturbing: science and parascience are mixed, above all on the level of the image. The *Encyclopedia* constantly proceeds to an impious fragmentation of the world, but what it finds at the term of this fracture is not the fundamental state of pure causes; in most cases the image obliges it to recompose an object that is strictly *unreasonable;* once the first nature is dissolved, another nature appears, quite as formed as the first. In a word, the fracture of the world is impossible: a glance suffices—ours— for the world to be eternally complete.

(1964)

Chateaubriand:
Life of Rancé

I am no longer anything but time.
—LIFE OF RANCÉ

Has anyone ever read the *Life of Rancé* as it was written, at least explicitly, i.e., as a work of penitence and edification? What can this biography of a Trappist in the age of Louis XIV written by a romantic have to say to an unbeliever, trained by his century not to yield to the glamor of "phrases"? Yet we can love this book, it can afford the sensation of a masterpiece, or better still (for that is too contemplative a notion) of a white-hot book in which some of us may rediscover certain problems, which is to say, certain limits, of our own. How can the pious work of an old rhetorician, written at the insistent behest of his confessor, looming up out of that French romanticism with which our modernity feels little affinity—how can this work concern us, astonish us, fulfill us? This kind of distortion, afforded by the time between writing and reading, is the very challenge of what we call literature: the work read is *anachronic,* and this anachronism is the crucial question it puts to the critic: we manage, little by little, to explain a work by its time or by its project, i.e., to justify the scandal of its appearance; but how reduce that of its survival? To what, then, can the *Life of Rancé* convert us, we who have read Marx, Nietzsche, Freud, Sartre, Genet, or Blanchot?

[41]

The Region of Deep Silence

Chateaubriand writes the *Life of Rancé* at seventy-six; it is his last work (he will die four years later). Which is a good position to develop a commonplace (in the technical sense of the term: a *topos*) of classical literature, that of the vanity of all things: transitory himself, at his journey's end, the old man can only sing what is passing: love, glory, in short, the world. This theme of *vanitas* is not alien to the *Life of Rancé;* often we seem to be reading *Ecclesiastes: "Societies long since vanished, how many others have followed you! the dancing floors are built upon the dust of the dead, and the graves grow beneath the steps of joy . . . Where are yesterday's troubles today? Where will today's pleasures be tomorrow?"* We thus encounter here, among incessant digressions, the classic apparatus of human vanities: fading loves (see the famous passage on love letters), graves, ruins (Rome), abandoned palaces (Chambord), perishing dynasties, invading forests, lovely women forgotten, the aging lionesses whose graves we can scarcely hear closing over them; perhaps for Chateaubriand alone this book does not wither.

Yet the sapiential theme, so frequent in classical and Christian literature, has virtually disappeared from modern works: old age is no longer a literary age; the old man is very rarely a novelistic hero; today it is the child who moves us, the adolescent who seduces, who disturbs; there is no longer any image of the old, no longer a philosophy of old age, perhaps because the old man is *undesirable.* Yet such an image can be lacerating, infinitely more than that of the child and quite as much as that of the adolescent, with whom the old man shares, moreover, the existential situation of abandonment; the *Life of Rancé,* whose obvious subject is old age, can move us quite as much as a love story, for old age (that long torment, as Michelet called it) can be a disease like love: Chateaubriand made a sickness of his old age (and this is new in relation to the classical *topos*); in him old age has a consistency of its own, it exists as a foreign body, awkward, painful, and the old man sustains certain magical relations with it: an incessant and varied metaphor furnishes it with a veritable substance, endowed with a color (it is the *nighttime traveler*) and a song (it is *the region of deep silence*). This languor of being old, deployed throughout the *Mémoires d'outretombe*, is here condensed in the figure of a solitary, Rancé; for one who voluntarily abandons the world can readily identify himself with one whom the world abandons: the dream, without which there would be no writing, abolishes any distinction between active and passive voices: abandoner and abandoned are here merely the same man, Chateaubriand can be Rancé.

At twenty-nine, before his conversion, Chateaubriand had written: *"Let us die utterly and altogether, lest we suffer elsewhere. This life must correct our rage for being."* Old age is a time when we die halfway, it is death without nothingness. This paradox has another name: Boredom (of Mme de Rambouillet growing old: "For a long time now she had no longer existed, barring the days which bore"); boredom is the expression of a time in excess, of a life in excess. In this dereliction, which is sung throughout the *Life of Rancé* under cover of piety (God is a convenient means for speaking of nothingness), we recognize an adolescent theme: *life was inflicted on me—What am I doing in the world?;* by this profoundly existential (and even existentialist) sentiment, the *Life of Rancé,* under its Christian panoply, suggests *Nausea;* the two experiences, moreover, have the same outcome: *writing:* only writing can give meaning to the insignificant; the difference is that our existential dereliction is inflicted on man metaphysically, beyond the ages; whereas Chateaubriand is in excess in relation to a previous time, to an existence of his memories; when memory appears as a complete system of representations (as is the case with the

Mémoires), life is ended, old age begins, which is of the order of pure time *(I am no longer anything but time)*; existence, then, is not regulated by physiology but by memory; once memory can coordinate, can structure (and this can happen when one is very young), existence becomes destiny, but thereby comes to an end, for destiny can never be conjugated except in the past-perfect historic, it is a closed tense. As the gaze which transforms it into destiny, old age makes life into an essence, but it is no longer life. This paradoxical situation makes the man who lives on into old age a double being (Chateaubriand speaks of Rancé's *bygone life*), who never attains to a complete existence: first the chimeras, then the memories, but never actual possession: this is the final impasse of old age: things are only when they are no longer: *"Bygones, you will not be reborn; and if you were, would you recover the charm with which you have decked out your dust?"* Anamnesis, which is ultimately the great subject of *Rancé,* for the Reformer, too, had a double life, worldly and monastic—anamnesis, then, is an operation both exalting and lacerating; this passion of memory is slaked only in an act which finally gives memory the stability of an essence: *writing.* Old age is for Chateaubriand closely linked to the idea of a work. His *Life of Rancé* is prophetically experienced as his last work, and twice over, he identifies himself with Poussin dying in Rome (the city of ruins) and depositing in his last painting that mysterious and sovereign imperfection, lovelier than a merely fulfilled art and which is *the tremor of time:* memory is the beginning of writing, and writing is in its turn the beginning of death (however young one is when one undertakes it).

Such, it appears, is the initiating experience of the *Life of Rancé:* an unhappy passion, that not of aging but of *being* old, having completely passed over to the side of pure time, in that region of profound silence (writing is not speaking) from which the true self seems remote, anterior (Chateaubriand measures his misery by the fact that he can henceforth *quote himself*). We understand that such an initiation has obliged Chateaubriand to introduce himself unceasingly into the Reformer's life, though he meant to be no more than his pious biographer. This kind of interlacing is banal enough: how recount someone without projecting yourself into him? But precisely: Chateaubriand's intervention is, in fact, not at all projective (or at least his project is very special); of course, there exist certain resemblances between Rancé and Chateaubriand; not to mention a common "stature," Rancé's worldly retreat (his conversion) doubles the separation from the world imposed (mythically) upon Chateaubriand by old age: both have a *bygone life*; but Rancé's is deliberately mute, in him memory (of his brilliant, literary, amorous youth) can speak, indeed, only in Chateaubriand's voice—Chateaubriand must remember for two; whence the intermingling, not of sentiments (Chateaubriand actually feels little sympathy for Rancé), but of memories. Chateaubriand's interference in Rancé's life is therefore not at all diffuse, sublime, imaginative, in a word "romantic" (in particular, Chateaubriand does not *distort* Rancé in order to lodge himself in him), but quite the contrary, broken, abrupt. Chateaubriand does not project himself, he superimposes himself, but since this discourse is apparently linear and since any operation of simultaneity is difficult for him, the author can do no more here than enter by force, fragmentarily, a life which is not his own; the *Life of Rancé* is not so much a cast, a broken work (we love its continuous "fall"); unceasingly, though each time briefly, the Reformer's thread is broken for the sake of the narrator's sudden reminiscence: Rancé arrives at Comminges after an earthquake: that was how Chateaubriand arrived at Grenada; Rancé translates St. Dorotheus: Chateaubriand has seen, between Jaffa and Gaza, the desert where the saint lived; Bossuet and Rancé walked together at La Trappe after vespers: "*I dared profane, with the steps which served me to dream René, the dike where Bossuet and Rancé spoke to one another of divine matters"*; St. Jerome, seeking to drown his thoughts in his sweats, carried weights of sand along the edge of the Red Sea: *"I traversed them myself, those plains, under the weight of my mind."* In this broken recurrence, which is the contrary of an assimilation and consequently, according to current meaning, of a "creation," there is something unsatisfied, a strange sort of undertow: the *self* is unforgettable: without ever absorbing him, Rancé periodically reveals Chateaubriand: never has an author undone himself less; in this *Life* there is something hard, made up of splinters, of fragments combined but not melted down; Chateaubriand does not double Rancé, he interrupts him, thereby prefiguring a literature of the fragment, according to which the inexorably separated consciousnesses (that of the author, that of the character) no longer hypocritically borrow the same composite voice. With Chateaubriand, the author begins his solitude: the author *is not* his character: a distance is established, which Chateaubriand assumes, without resigning himself to it; whence those reversals which give the *Life of Rancé* its special vertigo.

The Severed Head

Indeed, the *Life of Rancé* is composed in an irregular manner; of course, the four main parts follow chronology by and large: Rancé's worldly youth, his conversion, his life at La Trappe, his death; but if we descend to the level of those mysterious units of discourse still so ill defined by stylistics, intermediary between the word and the chapter (sometimes a sentence, sometimes a paragraph), the fracture of meaning is continual, as if Chateaubriand could never keep from suddenly turning his head toward "something else" (then is the writer *distracted?*); this disorder is apparent in the presentation of the portraits (very numerous in the *Life of Rancé*); we never know at which moment Chateaubriand is going to speak about someone; the digression is unforeseeable, its relation to the thread of the narrative is always abrupt and tenuous; thus, Chateaubriand has had several occasions to speak of the Cardinal de Retz at the moment of Rancé's Fronde-haunted youth; yet Retz's portrait emerges only long after the Fronde, during one of Rancé's journeys to Rome. Apropos of this seventeenth century he so admired, Chateaubriand speaks of *those times when nothing was yet classified,* thereby suggesting the profound *baroque* of our classicism. The *Life of Rancé* also participates in a certain *baroque* (we employ this word without any historical rigor), insofar as the author is willing to combine elements without structuring them according to the classical canon; in Chateaubriand there is an exaltation of rupture and of ramification. Though this phenomenon is not strictly speaking stylistic, since it may exceed the limits of the simple sentence, we can give it a rhetorical model: the *anacoluthon,* which is at once a break in construction and the explosion of a new meaning.

We know that, in ordinary discourse, the relation of words is subject to a certain probability. This ordinary probability is rarified by Chateaubriand; what likelihood is there of seeing the word *seaweed* appear in the life of Marcelle de Castellane? Yet Chateaubriand tells us all of a sudden, apropos of this young woman's death: *"The girls of Brittany let themselves drown on the beaches after having tied themselves to the seaweed of a rock."* The young Rancé is a prodigy in his Greek studies: what relation to the word *glove?* Yet, in two words, the relation is made explicit (the Jesuit Caussin tests the boy by hiding his text under his gloves). Through this cultivated gap, it is always a surprising substance *(seaweed, glove)* which erupts into the discourse. Literary language (since that is what is concerned here) thereby appears as an enormous and sumptuous debris, the fragmentary residue of an Atlantis where the words, overfed on color, on shape, in short on *qualities* and not on ideas, shine like the splinters of a *direct,* unthought world which no logic can manage to dim, to vex: that words should hang like lovely fruits on the indifferent tree of narrative, such is this writer's ultimate dream; we might assign as his symbol the stupefying anacoluthon whereby Chateaubriand speaks of orange trees apropos of Retz (*"at Saragossa he saw a priest walking alone because he had buried a plague-ridden parishioner. At Valencia, orange trees formed the highway fences, Retz breathed the air once breathed by Vannozia"*). The same sentence conducts several worlds (Retz, Spain) without taking the slightest pains to link them. By these sovereign anacoluthons the discourse is, in fact, established according to a certain depth: human speech seems to recall, to invoke, to receive another language (that of the gods, as is said in the *Cratylus*). The anacoluthon is, in fact, in and of itself, an order, a *ratio,* a principle; Chateaubriand's perhaps initiates a new logic, a very modern logic whose operator is the word's exclusive and extreme rapidity, without which the dream could not have invested our literature. This wild parataxis, this silence of the articulations, has, of course, the greatest consequences for the general economy of meaning: the anacoluthon obliges us to *seek out* meaning, it makes meaning "shudder" without determining it; from Retz to the orange trees of Valencia, meaning prowls but does not come to rest; a new break, a new explosion carries us on to Majorca, where Retz *"heard pious girls at a convent grille: they were singing"*: what connection? In literature, everything is thus *given* to be understood, and yet, as in our life itself, there is *ultimately* nothing to understand.

Indeed the anacoluthon introduces us to a poetics of distance. We ordinarily believe that the literary effort consists in seeking out affinities, correspondences, similitudes, and that the writer's function is to *unite* man and Nature in a single world (this is what we might call his synesthetic function). Yet metaphor, a fundamental figure of literature, can also be understood as a powerful tool of disjunction; notably in Chateaubriand, where it abounds, metaphor represents the contiguity but also the incommunication of two worlds, of two floating languages, at once united and separated, as if one were never anything but the nostalgia for the other; the narrative furnishes literal elements (even forces them on us) which are, by metaphoric means, suddenly snatched up, carried off, severed, separated, then abandoned to the naturalness of the anecdote, while the new word, introduced, as we have seen, forcibly, without preparation, by means of a violent anacoluthon, suddenly presents an irreducible *elsewhere.* Chateaubriand speaks of the smile of a dying young monk: *"It was as if one were hearing that nameless bird which consoles the traveler in the vale of Kashmir."* And in another place: *"Who was born, who dying, who weeping here? Silence! Birds high in the sky take wing for other climes."* In Chateaubriand, the metaphor never brings objects closer together, it separates worlds; technically (for it is the same thing, to talk of technique or metaphysics), we would say nowadays that the metaphor does not bear on a single signifier (as in the poetic comparison), but that, extended to the major units of discourse, it participates in the very life of the syntagm, which the linguists tell us is always very close to speech. Goddess of the division of things, Chateaubriand's great metaphor is always nostalgic; even while seeming to multiply resonances, it leaves man somehow *matte* in nature, and finally spares him the bad faith of a *direct* authenticity: for instance, it is impossible to speak humbly of oneself; Chateaubriand, by an ultimate ruse, without solving this impossibility, transcends it by taking us elsewhere: *"For myself, fond as I may be of my puny person, I know perfectly well I shall not exceed my own life. There have been unearthed, on Norwegian isles, some urns engraved with indecipherable characters. To whom do these ashes belong? The winds tell nothing."* Chateaubriand knows he *will* "exceed" his life; but it is not an impossible humility he wants to make us hear; what the urn, Norway, and the wind whisper to us is something nocturnal, something snowy, a certain hard, gray, cold desolation, in short, *something other* than oblivion, which is its simple anagogical meaning. Literature is, in short, never anything but a certain obliquity, *in which we get lost;* it separates, it deflects. Consider the death of Mme de Lamballe: *"Her life flew away like that sparrow on the Rhône ferry that, mortally wounded, makes the overloaded skiff list with its struggles";* which takes us oddly far from the Revolution.

Such, it would seem, is the major function of rhetoric and its figures: to make us understand, *at the same time,* something else. That the *Life of Rancé* is a literary work (and not, or not merely, apologetic) takes us very far from religion, and here the detour is once again assumed by a figure: antithesis. Antithesis is, according to Rousseau, as old as language; but in the *Life of Rancé,* which it structures completely, antithesis serves not only a demonstrative design (faith *overturns* lives), it is a veritable "renewal right" the writer has over time. Living out his own old age as a form, Chateaubriand could not be content with Rancé's "objective" conversion; in giving this life the form of a controlled speech (that of literature), the biographer had to divide it into a (worldly) *before* and a (solitary) *after,* proper to an infinite series of oppositions; for these oppositions to be rigorous, they had to be separated by a punctual, thin, sharp, and decisive event, like the crest of a mountain peak from which two different landscapes fall away; Chateaubriand found this event in the decapitation of Rancé's mistress; lover, author, soldier—in short, a man of the world, Rancé returns from hunting one evening, perceives his mistress's head beside her coffin, and veers immediately without a word into the fiercest possible religion: he thereby performs the very operation of contrariety, in its form and its abstraction. The event is thus, *literally,* poetic (*"All the poets have adopted Larroque's version*—which is the decapitation hypothesis—*all the religious commentators have rejected it*"); it is possible, one may say, only in literature; it is neither true nor false, it belongs to a system, without which there would be no *Life of Rancé,* or at least, by degrees, without which the *Life of Rancé* would concern neither Chateaubriand nor those remote readers who are ourselves. Literature thus substitutes an eternal plausibility for a contingent truth; for Rancé's conversion to win over time, our time, it must lose its own duration: in order to be *said,* it must happen all at once. This is why no object confided to language can be dialectical: the third term—time —is always missing: antithesis is the only possible survival of history. If *"the destiny of a great man is a Muse,"* she must speak by means of tropes.

The Abbé Séguin's Yellow Cat

In his preface, Chateaubriand tells us about his confessor, the Abbé Séguin, on whose orders, as a penitential labor, he has written the *Life of Rancé.* The Abbé Séguin had a yellow cat. Perhaps this yellow cat is literature itself, for if the notation doubtless refers to the idea that a yellow cat is an ill-favored, probably stray cat and thereby combines with other details of the Abbé's life, all attesting to his kindness and poverty, this yellow is also quite simply yellow, it leads not only to a sublime—in short, intellectual—meaning, it stubbornly remains on the level of colors (opposing, for example, the *black* of the old housekeeper, and that of the crucifix): to say a *yellow cat* and not a *stray cat* is in a way the act which separates writer from mere scribe, not because the yellow "creates an image," but because it casts a certain enchantment on the intentional meaning, returns speech to a kind of *asymptote* of meaning; the *yellow cat* says the Abbé Séguin's kindness, but also it says *less,* and it is here that there appears the scandal of literary speech. This speech is somehow endowed with a double wavelength; the longer one is that of meaning (the Abbé Séguin is a holy man, he lives in poverty accompanied by a stray cat); the shorter one transmits no information, if not literature itself: this is the more mysterious one, for because of it we cannot reduce literature to an entirely decipherable system: reading, criticism are not pure hermeneutics.

Concerned all his life by subjects which are not strictly literary—politics, religion, travel—Chateaubriand was nonetheless all his life a writer in the full sense and status: he immediately converted his (youthful) religious conversion into literature *(Le Génie du Christianisme);* as he did his political convictions, his sufferings, his life; he fully accommodated to our language that second wavelength which suspends speech between meaning and nonsense. Of course this prose-as-spectacle (the *epidictic,* as the Greeks called it) is very old, it prevails in all our classics, for as soon as rhetoric no longer serves judiciary purposes (which are its origins), it can no longer refer to anything but itself and literature begins, i.e., a mysteriously tautological language; yet Chateaubriand helps in instituting a new economy of rhetoric. Until very late in our literature, speech-as-spectacle (that of the classic writers, for instance) was always accompanied by a recourse to a traditional system of subjects (of *arguments*), which were called the topic. We have seen how Chateaubriand transformed the *topos* of *vanitas,* and how old age had become an existential theme for him; thus, there appeared in literature a new problem, or, if one prefers, a new form: the marriage of authenticity and spectacle. But also the impasse tightens.

The *Life of Rancé* represents this impasse very nicely. Rancé is an absolute Christian; as such, according to his own words, he must be *without memory, without recollection, and without resentment;* one might add: without literature. Of course the Abbé de Rancé wrote (certain religious works); he even had an author's coquetries (pulling a manuscript out of the flames); his religious conversion was nonetheless a writer's suicide; in his youth, Rancé had loved letters, had even distinguished himself in them; having become a monk and traveling, he *"neither writes nor keeps a journal"* (Chateaubriand notes). Yet to this literary death, Chateaubriand must give a literary life: this is the paradox of the *Life of Rancé* and this paradox is a general one, taking us far beyond a problem of conscience posed by a religion of abnegation. Every man who writes (and, therefore, who reads) has in him a Rancé and a Chateaubriand; Rancé tells him that his *self* cannot endure the theater of any language, or he is lost: to say *I* is inevitably to open a curtain, not so much to expose (which henceforth matters very little) as to inaugurate the ceremonial of the imaginary; Chateaubriand, for his part, tells him that the sufferings, the discomforts, the exaltations of this self, in short, the pure sentiment of his existence, can only plunge into language, that the "sensitive" soul is doomed to speech, and consequently to the very theater of that speech. For nearly two centuries this contradiction has haunted our writers: consequently we find ourselves dreaming of a pure writer who does not write. This is obviously not a moral problem, not a matter of siding with or against a fatal ostentation of language; on the contrary, it is language, as Kierkegaard saw, which, being the general, represents the category of the ethical, since to be absolutely individual, Abraham doing sacrifice must renounce language; he is condemned not to speak. The modern writer is and is not Abraham: he must be at once outside the ethical and within language; he must create the general with the irreducible, rediscover the amorality of his existence through the moral generality of language: it is this *hazardous* passage which is literature.

What is it for? What does it accomplish to say *yellow cat* instead of *stray cat?* or to call old age *the nighttime traveler?* or to speak of the fences of orange trees in Valencia apropos of Cardinal de Retz? What use is the severed head of the Duchess of Montbazon? Why transform Rancé's (already suspect) humility into a spectacle endowed with all the ostentation of style (the character's style of being, the writer's verbal style)? This group of operations, this *technique,* whose (social) incongruity we can never escape, may serve this purpose: *to suffer less.* We do not know whether Chateaubriand received some pleasure, some comfort, from having written the *Life of Rancé;* but reading this work, and although Rancé himself is indifferent to us, we understand the power of a useless language. Certainly calling old age *the nighttime traveler* cannot continuously cure the misery of growing old; for on the one hand, there is the time of real miseries which cannot have any issue but a dialectical (i.e., an unnamed) one; and on the other, some metaphor which explodes, which enlightens without acting. And yet this explosion of the word affords our wretchedness the shock of a distance: the new form is a kind of lustral bath for our suffering: worn down since its origin within language (are there any sentiments besides those which are named?), it is nonetheless language—but *another* language—which renews the pathetic. This distance, established by writing, should have only one name (if we could dispense with its harsh connotation): *irony.* In relation to the difficulty of being, of which it is a continual observation, the *Life of Rancé* is a work of sovereign irony *(eironeia* means *interrogation);* we might define it as a nascent schizophrenia, prudently formed in a homeopathic quantity: is it not a certain "detachment" applied by the excess of words (all writing is emphatic) to the tenacious will to suffer?

(1965)

Proust
and Names

W e know that *Remembrance of Things Past* is the story of a writing. It may be useful to recall this story, the better to understand how it *comes out*, since this outcome represents what, ultimately, permits the writer to write.

The birth of a book which we shall not know (but whose harbinger is Proust's own book) functions as a drama in three acts. The first act sets forth the will to write: the young narrator perceives this will in himself through the erotic pleasure Bergotte's sentences afford him and the joy he experiences describing the steeples of Martinville. The second act—a very long one, since it occupies the essential part of *Remembrance*—deals with the inability to write. This inability is articulated in three scenes or, one might say, three distresses: first, Norpois affords the young narrator a discouraging image of literature: a ridiculous image, though one he may not even have the talent to fulfill; then, much later, a second image will depress him further: a rediscovered passage from the Goncourt *Journal*, at once glamorous and laughable, confirms in him, by comparison, his own impotence to transform sensation into notation; lastly, more serious still because bearing on his very sensibility and no longer on his talent, a final incident dissuades him from writing for good: taking the train to Paris after a long illness, the narrator observes three trees in the countryside and experiences only indifference before their beauty; he concludes that he will never write; sadly liberated from every obligation toward a vow he is decidedly incapable of fulfilling, he decides to return to the world's frivolity and attends an afternoon party at the Duchess de Guermantes's. Here, by a truly dramatic reversal, having drunk the very lees of renunciation, the narrator will rediscover, under his hand, the power to write. This third act occupies all of *The Past Recaptured* and also includes three episodes; the first consists of three successive fits of vertigo: these are three reminiscences (St. Mark's, the trees from the train, Balbec), looming out of three trivial incidents during his arrival at the Hôtel de Guermantes (the uneven paving stones of the courtyard, the noise of a little spoon, a starched napkin handed him by a servant); these reminiscences are felicities which must now be understood if they are to be preserved, or at least recalled, at will: in a second episode, which forms the essential part of the Proustian theory of literature, the narrator systematically devotes himself to exploring the signs he has received and thereby to understanding, in a single impulse, the world and the Book, the Book as world and the world as Book. A final suspension, however, postpones the power to write: examining the guests he had lost sight of for so long, the narrator is stupefied to perceive that they have aged: Time, which has restored writing to him, risks at the same moment snatching it from him: will he live long enough to write his work? Yes, if he agrees to withdraw from the world, to lose his worldly life in order to save his life as a writer.

The story told by the narrator thus has all the dramatic characteristics of an initiation; it involves a veritable mystagogy, articulated in three dialectical movements: desire (the mystagogue postulates a revelation), failure (he assumes dangers, darkness, nothingness), assumption (it is at failure's climax that he finds victory). Now, in order to write *Remembrance*, Proust himself experienced, in his own life, this initiatic pattern: the precocious desire to write (formed as early as his *lycée* years) was followed by a long period not of failures but of groping, as if the true and unique work were being sought, abandoned, resumed, without ever being found; and like the narrator's, this negative initiation, so to speak, was accomplished through a certain experience of literature: other men's books fascinated, then disappointed Proust, just as those of Bergotte or the Goncourts fascinated and disappointed the narrator; this passage through literature, so similar to the trajectory of initiations, filled with darkness and illusions, was accomplished by means of parody and pastiche (what better testimony to fascination and demystification than pastiche?), of desperate infatuation (Ruskin) and contestation (Sainte-Beuve). Proust thus approached *Remembrance* (of which, as we know, certain fragments already occur in his *Contre Sainte-Beuve*), but the work did not manage to "take." The main units were there (relationships of characters[1] crystallizing episodes[2]) being tested in various combinations, as in a kaleidoscope, but still missing was that federating act which would permit Proust to write *Remembrance* without flagging, from 1909 to his death, at the cost of a retreat which so resembles, as we know, that of the narrator himself at the end of *The Past Recaptured*.

We shall not attempt here to explain Proust's work by his life; we shall concern ourselves only with acts internal to the discourse itself (consequently, poetic and not biographical acts), whether this discourse be the narrator's or Marcel

---

[1]For instance: the inopportune visitor of the Combray evenings, who will be Swann; the lover of the little band of girls, who will be the narrator.

[2]For instance, the morning reading of *Le Figaro*, brought to the narrator by his mother.

Proust's. Now the homology which, from all evidence, governs the two discourses calls for a symmetrical denouement: the establishment of writing by reminiscence (in the narrator) must correspond (in Proust) to some similar discovery likely to establish, in its imminent continuity, all the writing of *Remembrance*. What, then, is the accident—not biographical, but creative—which gathers together a work already conceived, tested, but not quite written? What is the new cement which will grant syntagmatic unity to so many scattered, discontinuous units? What is it which permits Proust to utter his work? In a word, what does the writer find, symmetrical to the reminiscences the narrator had explored and exploited during the Guermantes party?

The two discourses, the narrator's and Marcel Proust's, are homologous but not analogous. The narrator is *going* to write, and this future maintains him in an order of existence, not of speech; he is at grips with a psychology, not with a technique. Marcel Proust, on the contrary, writes; he struggles with the categories of language, not with those of behavior. Belonging to the referential world, reminiscence cannot be directly a unit of discourse, and what Proust needs is a strictly poetic element (in the sense Jakobson gives to the word); but also this linguistic feature, like reminiscence, must have the power to constitute the essence of novelistic objects. Now there is a class of verbal units which possesses to the highest degree this constitutive power, and this class is that of proper names. The proper name possesses the three properties which the narrator concedes to reminiscence: the power of essentialization (since one "unfolds" a proper name exactly as one does a memory): the proper name is in a sense the linguistic form of reminiscence. Therefore, the (poetic) event which "launched" *Remembrance* is the discovery of Names; doubtless, since his *Contre Sainte-Beuve,* Proust already possessed certain names *(Combray, Guermantes);* but it was only between 1907 and 1909, it appears, that he constituted in its entirety the onomastic system of *Remembrance:* once this system was found, the work was written immediately.[1]

Proust's work describes an immense, an incessant apprenticeship.[2] This apprenticeship always knows two moments (in love, in art, in worldliness): an illusion and a disappointment; from these two moments is born the truth, i.e., writing; but between dream and waking, before the truth appears, the Proustian narrator must perform an ambiguous task (for it leads to the truth through many misunderstandings), which consists in desperately interrogating the signs: signs emitted by the work of art, by the beloved, by the milieu frequented. The proper name is also a sign, and not of course a simple index which would designate without signifying, according to the current conception from Peirce to Russell. As sign, the proper name offers itself to an exploration, a decipherment: it is at once a "milieu" (in the biological sense of the term) into which one must plunge, steeping in all the reveries it bears,[3] and a precious object, compressed, embalmed, which must be opened like a flower.[4] In other words, if the Name (as we shall henceforth call the proper name) is a sign, it is a voluminous sign, a sign always pregnant with a dense texture of meaning, which no amount of wear can reduce, can flatten, contrary to the common noun, which releases only

---

[1]Proust has given his theory of the proper noun twice over: in *Contre Sainte-Beuve* (Chapter 14: "Names of Persons") and in *Swann's Way* ("Place names: the Name").

[2]This is the thesis of Gilles Deleuze in his remarkable book *Proust and Signs.*

[3]"Not thinking of the names as an inaccessible ideal, but as a real ambiance into which I would plunge" *(Swann's Way).*

[4]". . . Delicately to remove the wrappings of habit and to see again in its first freshness this name *Guermantes* . . ." *(Contre Sainte-Beuve).*

one of its meanings by syntagm. The Proustian Name is in itself and in every case the equivalent of an entire dictionary column: the name *Guermantes* immediately covers everything that memory, usage, culture can put into it; it knows no selective restriction, the syntagm in which it is placed is indifferent to it; it is, therefore, in a certain fashion, a semantic monstrosity, for, provided with all the characteristics of the common noun, it can nonetheless exist and function outside of any projective rule. This is the price—or the ransom—of the phenomenon of "hypersemanticity" of which it is the seat,[1] and which closely relates it, of course, to the poetic word.

By its semantic density (one would almost like to be able to say, its *lamination*), the Proustian Name offers itself to a veritable semic analysis, which the narrator himself does not fail to postulate or to sketch out: what he calls the Name's different "figures"[2] are veritable semes, endowed with a perfect semantic validity, despite their imaginary character (which proves once more how necessary it is to distinguish the signified from the referent). The name *Guermantes* thus contains several *primitives* (to borrow a word from Leibniz): "*a castle keep without density, which was nothing but a strip of orange-tinted light and at the top of which the lord and his lady decided the life or the death of their vassals*"; "*a yellowing and rosetted tower which traverses the ages*"; the Parisian mansion of the Guermantes, "*limpid as its name*"; a feudal castle in the middle of Paris, etc. These semes are, of

---

[1]Cf. U. Weinreich, "On the Semantic Structure of Language," in J. H. Greenberg, *Universals of Language.*

[2]"But later, I find in the duration of this same name within myself, seven or eight different figures one after the other . . ." *(The Guermantes Way).*

course, "images," but in the higher language of literature, they are no less pure signifieds, offered like those of the denotating language to a whole systematics of meaning. Certain of these semic images are traditional, cultural: *Parma* does not designate an Emilian city situated on the Po, founded by the Etruscans, and comprising 138,000 inhabitants; the true signified of these two syllables is composed of two semes: Stendhalian sweetness and the reflection of violets *(Swann's Way)*. Others are individual, memorial: *Balbec* has as its semes two words spoken long ago to the narrator, one by Legrandin (Balbec is a stormy place at the end of the earth), the other by Swann (its church is half Norman gothic, half Romanesque), so that the Name always has two simultaneous meanings: "Gothic architecture and a storm at sea" *(Swann's Way)*. Thus, each Name has its semic specter, variable in time, according to the chronology of its reader, who adds or subtracts elements exactly as language does in its diachrony. The Name is, in effect, *catalyzable;* it can be filled, dilated, the interstices of its semic armature can be infinitely added to. This semic dilation of the proper name can be defined in another way: each Name contains several "scenes" appearing at first in a discontinuous, erratic manner, but which ask only to be federated and to form thereby a little narrative, for to recount is never anything but to link together, by metonymic processes, a limited number of complete units: *Balbec* thus conceals not only several scenes but also the movement which can collect them together in one and the same narrative syntagm, for its heteroclite syllables were doubtless generated by an archaic way of pronouncing, *"which I did not expect I would ever encounter until my arrival, when the innkeeper would serve me* café au lait *and then take me to see the sea flinging itself against the walls of the church, and to whom I lent the argumentative, solemn and medieval aspect of a character out of an old French romance" (Swann's Way).* It is because the Name offers itself to an infinitely rich catalysis that it can be said that, poetically, the whole of *Remembrance* emerges from a few names *("This* Guermantes *was something like the plot of a novel: The Guermantes Way).*

Yet they must be carefully chosen—or found. Here there appears, in the Proustian theory of the Name, a major problem, if not of linguistics, at least of semiology: the motivation of the sign. Doubtless this problem is somewhat artificial, since it actually comes up only for the novelist, who has the freedom (but also the obligation) to create proper names at once new and yet "exact"; but as it happens the narrator and the novelist cover the same trajectory in contrary directions: the narrator believes he can decipher, in the names given to him, a kind of natural affinity between signifier and signified, between the vocalic color of *Parma* and the mauve sweetness of its content; the novelist, having to invent a site at once Norman, Gothic, and windy, must search the general tablature for phonemes, a few sounds tuned to the combination of these signifieds; one decodes, the other encodes, but the same system is involved and this system is, one way or another, a motivated system, based on a relation of *imitation* between signifier and signified. Encoder and decoder might here adopt for themselves Cratylus's assertion: *"The name's property consists in representing the thing as it is."* According to Proust, who merely theorizes the novelist's art in general, the proper name is a simulation or, as Plato said (with mistrust, it is true), a "fantasmagoria."

The motivations Proust alleges are of two kinds, natural and cultural. The former derive from symbolic phonetics (Weinreich has noted that phonetic symbolism derives from the sign's hypersemanticity). This is not the place to continue the argument on this question (once known under the name of *imitative harmony*), where we would find, among others, the names of Plato, Leibniz, Diderot, and Jakobson. We shall merely cite this text by Proust, less famous than but perhaps as pertinent as Rimbaud's "Sonnet of the Vowels": "... *Bayeux, so high in its noble reddish lace and whose crest is illuminated by the old gold of its last syllable; Vitré, whose acute accent lozenged the old stained glass with black wood; mild Lamballe whose whiteness shades from eggshell to pearl gray; Coutances, a Norman cathedral whose final diphthong, fat and yellowing, crowns it with a tower of butter,*" etc. (*Swann's Way*. We may note that the motivation asserted by Proust is not only phonetic but also, sometimes, graphic.) Proust's examples, by their freedom and their richness (it is no longer a question of attributing to the *i/o* opposition the traditional contrast of *thin/round:* here it is an entire gamut of phonic signs which is described by Proust), indicate that in most cases phonetic motivation is not direct: the decoder intercalates between sound and meaning an intermediary concept, half material, half abstract, which functions as a key and opens the "narrowed" passage from signifier to signified: if *Balbec* signifies by affinity a complex of high-crested waves, steep cliffs, and bristling architecture, it is because we possess a conceptual relay, that of the word *rugueux* (rugose), which "works" for touch, hearing, and sight. In other words, the phonetic motivation requires an internal nomination: language surreptitiously returns to a relation which was mythically postulated as immediate: most apparent motivations are based on metaphors so traditional (the word *rugueux* applied to sound) that they are no longer perceived as such, having passed entirely to the side of denotation; nonetheless, motivation is determined at the cost of an old semantic anomaly or, one might say, of an old transgression. For it is obviously to metaphor that we must reattach the phenomena of symbolic phonetism, and it would be no use studying the one without the other. Proust would furnish good raw material for this

combined study: his phonetic motivations imply in almost
every case (except perhaps for *Balbec*) an equivalence between
sound and color: *ieu* is old gold, *é* is black, *an* is yellowing,
blond, and golden (in *Coutances* and *Guermantes*), *i* is purple.[1]
Here is an obviously general tendency: it is a question of
shifting to the aspect of sound certain features belonging to
sight (and more particularly to color, by reason of its simultaneously vibratory and modulating nature), i.e., in short, of
neutralizing the opposition of several virtual classes resulting
from the separation of senses (but is this separation historical
or anthropological? From what period and from where do our
"five senses" come? A renewed study of metaphor should
henceforth consider, it would seem, the inventory of the nominal classes attested to by general linguistics). All in all, if
phonetic motivation implies a metaphoric process, and consequently a transgression, this transgression occurs at tested
points of transition, such as color: it is for this reason, no
doubt, that the motivations Proust advances, while being very
highly developed, appear to be so "just."

There remains another type of motivation, more "cultural"
and thereby analogous to those we find in language: this type
governs in effect both the invention of neologisms, aligned on
a morphematic model, and the invention of proper names,
these "inspired" by a phonetic model. When a writer invents
a proper name, he is actually governed by the same rules of
motivation as Plato's legislator when he wants to create a
common noun: he must in a sense "copy" the thing and, since
this is obviously impossible, at least must copy the way in
which language itself has created certain of its names. The
equality of common and proper names before creation is

---

[1] "Sylvie's color is purple, reddish-purple, or a kind of violet velvet . . . And
this name itself, purple on account of its two *i*'s—Sylvie, the true Daughter
of Fire" *(Contre Sainte-Beuve)*.

nicely illustrated by an extreme case: that in which the writer pretends to employ ordinary words which nonetheless he makes up out of whole cloth: this is the case with Joyce and with Michaux; in the latter's *Voyage en Grande Garabagne*, a word like *arpette* has—and with good reason—no meaning but is nonetheless filled with a diffuse signification, by reason not only of its context but also of its subjection to a phonic model very common in French.[1] The same is true of the Proustian names. Whether or not *Laumes, Argencourt, Villeparisis, Combray*, or *Doncières* exist, they nonetheless possess (and this is what matters) what we may call a "Francophonic plausibility": their true signified is *France* or, better still, "Frenchness"; their phonetism, and at least to an equal degree their graphism, are elaborated in conformity with certain sounds and groups of letters specifically attached to French toponymy: it is culture (that of the French) which imposes upon the Name a natural motivation: what is imitated is of course not in Nature but in history, yet a history so old that it constitutes the language which has resulted from it as a veritable nature, the source of models and reasons. The proper name, and singularly the Proustian Name, therefore, has a common signification: it signifies at least the nationality and all the images which can be associated with it. It can even refer to more particular signifieds, such as the province (not so much as a region, but as a milieu), in Balzac, or as the social class, in Proust: not of course by the ennobling particle, a crude means, but by the institution of a broad onomastic system, articulated on the opposition of the aristocracy and the commonalty on the one hand, and on the opposition of long syllables with mute final *e*'s (final syllables provided, so to speak, with a long

---

[1] These invented words have been well analyzed from a linguistic point of view by Delphine Perret, in her Sorbonne thesis of 1966, *Étude de la langue littéraire d'après le Voyage en Grande Garabagne d'Henri Michaux*.

train) and abrupt short syllables: on one side the paradigm of
Guermantes, Laumes, Agrigente; on the other that of *Verdurin,
Morel, Jupien, Legrandin, Sazerat, Cottard, Brichot,* etc.[1]

Proustian onomastics seems so organized that it actually
constitutes, to all appearances, the definitive initiation of *Remembrance:* to possess a system of names was for Proust—and
is for us—to hold the essential significations of the book, the
armature of its signs, its profound syntax. We therefore see
that the Proustian Name fully wields the two major dimensions of the sign: on the one hand, it can be read all by itself
as a totality of significations (*Guermantes* contains several
figures), in short, as an essence (an "original entity," Proust
says), or if we prefer, an absence, since the sign designates
what is not there;[2] and on the other hand it sustains with its
congeners certain metonymic relations, establishes Narrative:
Swann and *Guermantes* are not only two paths, two ways, they
are also two phonetisms, like *Verdurin* and *Laumes.* If the
proper name in Proust has this ecumenical function, summarizing all of language, it is because its structure coincides with
that of the work itself: to advance gradually into the Name's
significations (as the narrator keeps doing) is to be initiated
into the world, to learn to decipher its essences: the signs of
the world (of love, of worldliness) consist of the same stages as
its names; between the thing and its appearance develops the
dream, just as between the referent and its signifier is inter-
posed the signified: the Name is nothing, if we should be so

---

[1]What is involved here is, of course, a tendency, not a law. Further, I am
using *long* and *short* syllables without phonetic rigor, but rather as an ordinary
impression, based moreover largely on the written forms, the French being
accustomed by their academic, essentially written culture, to perceive a tyran-
nical opposition between masculine rhymes and feminine rhymes, the former
perceived as short, the latter as long.

[2]"We can imagine only what is absent" *(The Past Recaptured).* We may
further recall that, for Proust, to imagine is to unfold a sign.

unfortunate as to articulate it directly on its referent (what, *in reality*, is the Duchess de Guermantes?), i.e., if we miss in it its nature as *sign*. The signified is thus the site of the imaginary: here, no doubt, is Proust's new thought, the reason why he has historically displaced the old problem of realism, which until his advent was always posed in terms of referents: the writer works not on the relation of the thing and its form (what was called, in classical times, his "painting" and, more recently, his "expression"), but on the relation of signified and signifier, i.e., on a sign. It is this relation of which Proust gives us the linguistic theory in his reflections on the Name and in the etymological discussions he entrusts to Brichot, which would have little meaning if the writer did not accord them an emblematic function.

These remarks are not only oriented by my concern to recall, after Claude Lévi-Strauss, the signifying and not the indicial character of the proper name. I also want to insist on the Cratylean character of the name (and of the sign) in Proust: not only because Proust sees the relation of signifier and signified as a motivated relation, one copying the other and reproducing in its material form the signified essence of the thing (and not the thing itself), but also because, for Proust as for Cratylus, "the virtue of names is to teach": there is a propaedeutics of names which leads, by paths often long, various, and indirect, to the essence of things. It is for this reason that no one is closer to the Cratylean Legislator, founder of names *(demiourgos onomatôn)*, than the Proustian writer, not because he is free to invent the names he likes, but because he is obliged to invent them "properly." This realism (in the scholastic sense of the term), which insists that names be the "reflection" of ideas, has taken a radical form in Proust, but we may speculate if it is not more or less consciously present in every act of writing and if it is really possible to be a writer without believing, in some sense, in the natural relation of names and essences: the poetic function, in the broadest sense of the term, would thus be defined by a Cratylean consciousness of signs and the writer would be the mouthpiece of a great age-old myth which decrees that language imitates ideas and that, contrary to the specifications of linguistic science, signs are motivated. This consideration should incline the critic still further to read literature in the mythic perspective which establishes its language and to decipher the literary word (which is never the word in common usage), not as the dictionary explicates it, but as the writer constructs it.

(1967)

Flaubert
and the Sentence

Long before Flaubert, writers had experienced—and expressed—the arduous labor of style, the exhaustion of incessant corrections, the sad necessity of endless hours committed to an infinitesimal output.[1] Yet in Flaubert, the dimension of this agony is altogether different; the labor of style is for him an unspeakable suffering (even if he speaks it quite often), an almost expiatory ordeal for which he acknowledges no compensation of a magical (i.e., aleatory) order, as the sentiment of inspiration might be for many writers: style, for Flaubert, is absolute suffering, infinite suffering, useless suffering. Writing is disproportionately slow *("four pages this week," "five days for a page," "two days to reach the end of two lines");* it requires an "irrevocable farewell to life," a pitiless sequestration; we may note in this regard that Flaubert's sequestration occurs uniquely for the sake of style, while Proust's, equally famous,

---

[1]Here are several examples from Antoine Albalat's book, *Le Travail du style, enseigné par les corrections manuscrites des grands écrivains* (1903): Pascal rewrote the XVIII Provincial Letter thirteen times; Rousseau worked on *Émile* for three years; Buffon worked more than ten hours a day; Chateaubriand would spend twelve to fifteen hours at a time rewriting, erasing, etc.

has for its object a total recuperation of the work: Proust
retires from the world because he has a great deal to say and
because he is pressed by death, Flaubert because he has an
infinite correction to perform; once sequestered, Proust adds
endlessly (his famous *"paperolles"*), Flaubert subtracts, erases,
constantly returns to zero, begins over again. Flaubertian sequestration has for its center (and its symbol) a piece of furniture which is not the desk but the divan: when the depths of
agony are plumbed, Flaubert throws himself on his sofa[1]: this
is his "marinade," an ambiguous situation, in fact, for the sign
of failure is also the site of fantasy, whence the work will
gradually resume, giving Flaubert a new substance which he
can erase anew. Flaubert qualifies this Sisyphean circuit by a
very strong word, *"atrocious,"*[2] the sole recompense he receives
for his life's sacrifice.[3]

Apparently, then, style engages the writer's entire existence, and for this reason it would be better to call it henceforth a *writing*: to write is to live *("A book has always been for
me,"* Flaubert says, *"a particular way of living"*), writing is the
book's goal, not publication.[4] This precellence, attested—or
purchased—by the very sacrifice of a life, somewhat modifies
the traditional conceptions of "writing well," ordinarily given
as the final garment (the ornament) of ideas or passions. First
of all, according to Flaubert, the very opposition of form and

---

[1]"Sometimes when I feel empty, when expression is refractory, when after
having scribbled many pages I discover I haven't made a single sentence, I fall
on my couch and lie there stupefied in an inner marsh of ennui" (1852).

[2]"One achieves style only by atrocious labor, a fanatic and dedicated stub-
bornness" (1846).

[3]"I have spent my life depriving my heart of its most legitimate nourish-
ment. I have led a laborious and austere existence. And now I can bear no
more, I am at the end of my tether" (1875).

[4]"... I don't want to publish anything ... I work with an absolute disinterestedness and without ulterior motive, without external preoccupation ..."
(1846).

content vanishes[1]: to write and to think are but one action, writing is a total being. Then comes, so to speak, the reversion of the merits of poetry over prose: poetry holds up to prose the mirror of its constraints, the image of a close-set, sure code: this model exerts an ambiguous fascination upon Flaubert, since prose must at once rejoin verse and exceed it, equal it and absorb it. Finally, there is a special distribution of technical tasks required by the elaboration of a novel; classical rhetoric focused on the problems of *dispositio,* or order of the parts of discourse (which we must not confuse with *compositio,* or order of the internal elements of the sentence); Flaubert seems not to be interested in this; he does not neglect the tasks proper to narration[2], but these tasks, evidently, have only a loose link with his essential project: to compose his work or any of its episodes is not "atrocious" but simply "wearisome."[3]

As an odyssey, Flaubertian writing (and how active a meaning we should like to give this word) thus confines itself to what we commonly call corrections of style. These corrections are not in any way rhetorical accidents; they affect the primary code, that of the language; they commit the writer to experiencing the structure of the language as a passion. Here we must prepare what we might call a linguistics (and not a stylistics) of corrections, somewhat symmetrical to what Henri Frei has called the grammar of mistakes.

The corrections writers make on their manuscripts may be

---

[1]"For me, insofar as you have not separated form from content in a given sentence, I maintain that these are actually two words devoid of meaning" (1846).

[2]See notably the account of the pages concerning various episodes of *Madame Bovary:* "I already have 260 pages which contain only preparations for action, more or less disguised expositions of characters (it is true that they are graduated), landscapes, places . . ."

[3]"I have a narration to compose; now the story is something which is very wearisome for me. I have to send my heroine to a ball" (1852).

readily classified according to the two axes of the paper on which they write; on the vertical axis are made the substitutions of words (these are the crossings out or "hesitations"); on the horizontal axis, the suppressions or additions of syntagms (these are the "recastings"). Now the axes of the paper are the very same thing as the axes of the language. The first corrections are substitutive, metaphorical; they tend to replace the sign initially inscribed by another sign chosen from a paradigm of affinitary and different elements; these corrections can then bear on the monemes (Hugo substituting *modest* for *charming* in *"Eden wakened, charming and nude"*) or on the phonemes, when it is a matter of prohibiting certain assonances (which classical prose does not tolerate) or overinsistent homophonies held to be absurd (in French the sound of *Après cet essai fait: cétécéfé*). The secondary corrections (corresponding to the horizontal order of the page) are associative, metonymic; they affect the syntagmatic chain of the message, modifying its volume by diminution or enlargement according to two rhetorical models: ellipsis and catalysis.

In short, the writer possesses three main types of corrections: substitutive, diminutive, and augmentative: he can work by permutation, subtraction, or expansion. Now these three types have not altogether the same status, and moreover they have not had the same fortune. Substitution and ellipsis bear on limited groups. The paradigm is closed by the constraints of distribution (which oblige the writer, in principle, to permute only terms of the same class) and by those of meaning, which require him to exchange affinitary terms.[1] As we cannot replace a sign by just any other sign, we also cannot reduce a

---

[1] We must not limit affinity to a purely analogical relation, and it would be wrong to suppose that writers permute only synonymous terms: a classical writer like Bossuet can substitute *laugh* for *weep:* the antonymous relation constitutes part of the affinity.

sentence indefinitely; the diminutive correction (ellipsis) eventually comes up against the irreducible cell of any sentence, the subject-predicate group (it will be understood that *in practical terms* the limits of ellipsis are often reached much sooner, by reason of various cultural constraints, such as eurhythmy, symmetry, etc.): ellipsis is limited by the structure of the language. This very structure permits us, on the contrary, to give free rein, without limit, to augmentative corrections; on the one hand, the parts of speech can be indefinitely multiplied (if only by digression), and on the other (this is what particularly interests us here), the sentence may be indefinitely furnished with interpolations and expansions: the catalytic work is theoretically infinite; even if the structure of the sentence is actually governed and limited by literary models (in the manner of poetical meter) or by physical constraints (the limits of human memory, relative moreover, since classical literature admits the *period*, virtually unknown to ordinary speech), it remains nonetheless true that the writer, confronting the sentence, experiences the infinite freedom of speech, as it is inscribed within the very structure of language. Hence what is involved is a problem of freedom, and we must note that the three types of corrections of which we have just spoken have not had the same fortune; according to the classical ideal of style, the writer is required to rework his substitutions and his ellipses tirelessly, by virtue of the correlative myths of the "exact word" and of "concision," both guarantees of "clarity,"[1] while he is discouraged from any labor of expansion; in classical manuscripts, permutations and crossings out abound, but we find virtually no augmentative

---

[1] It is a classical paradox—which in my opinion should be explored—that clarity should be given as the natural product of concision (see Mme Necker's remark, given in Brunot's *Histoire de la langue française:* "The shortest sentence is always preferable when it is also clear, *for it necessarily becomes more so*").

corrections except in Rousseau and above all in Stendhal, whose subversive attitude with regard to "fine style" is well known.

To return to Flaubert: the corrections he made on his manuscripts are doubtless varied, but if we abide by what he himself asserted and commented, the "atrocity" of style is concentrated in two points, which are the writer's two crosses. The first cross is the repetition of words; it is a matter of substitutive correction here, since it is the (phonic) form of the word whose too-immediate return must be avoided, while retaining the content; as we have said, the possibilities of correction are limited here, which should lighten the writer's responsibility all the more; yet here Flaubert manages to introduce the vertigo of an infinite correction: the difficulty, for him, is not correction itself (actually limited), but discernment of the place where it is necessary: certain repetitions appear, which had not been noticed the day before, so that nothing can guarantee that the next day new "mistakes" will not be discovered;[1] thus, there develops an anxious insecurity, for it always seems possible to *hear* new repetitions:[2] the text, even when it has been meticulously worked over, is somehow *mined* with risks of repetition: limited and consequently reassured in its act, substitution again becomes free and consequently agonizing by the infinity of its possible emplacements: the paradigm is of course closed, but since it functions with each significative unit, it is seized again by the infinity of the syntagm. The second cross of Flaubertian writing is the transi-

---

[1] Apropos of three pages of *Madame Bovary* (1853): "I will doubtless discover in them a thousand repetitions of words which I'll have to get rid of. At this moment, late as it is, I can see virtually none."

[2] This audition of a language within language (however erroneous) recalls another audition quite as vertiginous: that which permitted Saussure to hear a second, anagrammatic message in most verses of Greek, Latin, and Vedic poetry.

tions (or articulations) of the discourse.[1] As we might expect of a writer who has continuously absorbed content in form—or more precisely contested this very antinomy—the linking of ideas is not experienced directly as a logical constraint but must be defined in terms of the signifier; what is to be obtained is fluidity, the optimal rhythm of the course of speech, in a word *sequence,* that *flumen orationis* already demanded by the classical rhetoricians. Here Flaubert comes up against the problem of syntagmatic corrections once more: the good syntagm is an equilibrium between excessive forces of constriction and of dilatation; but whereas ellipsis is normally limited by the very structure of the sentential unit, Flaubert reintroduces an infinite freedom into it: once acquired, he turns it back and reorients it toward a new expansion: a matter of constantly "unscrewing" what is too tight: ellipsis now acquires the vertigo of expansion.[2]

For it is indeed a matter of vertigo: correction is infinite, it has no sure sanction. The corrective protocols are perfectly systematic—and in this they might be reassuring—but since their points of application are endless, no appeasement is possible:[3] they are groups at once structured and floating. Yet this vertigo does not have as its motif the infinity of discourse, the traditional field of rhetoric; it is linked to a linguistic object, known of course to rhetoric, at least from the moment when, with Dionysus of Halicarnassus and the anonymous author of

---

[1]"What is atrociously difficult is the linking of ideas, so that they derive naturally from each other" (1852). ". . . And then the transitions, the *sequence* —what an entanglement!" (1853).

[2]"Each paragraph is good in itself, and there are pages I am certain are perfect. But just because of this, *it doesn't work.* It's a series of well-turned paragraphs which do not lead into each other. I'm going to have to unscrew them, loosen the joints" (1853).

[3]"I ended by leaving off the corrections; I had reached the point where I understood nothing—pressing too hard on a piece of work, it dazzles you; what seems to be wrong now in five minutes seems perfectly all right" (1853).

On the Sublime, rhetoric had discovered "style," but to which Flaubert has given a technical and even metaphysical existence of an incomparable force, and which is *the sentence.*

For Flaubert, the sentence is at once a unit of style, a unit of work, and a unit of life; it attracts the essential quality of his confidences as his work as a writer.[1] If we rid the expression of any metaphorical resonance, we might say that Flaubert has spent his life "making sentences"; the sentence is, so to speak, the work's double *reflection,* it is on the level of the fabrication of sentences that the writer has created the history of this work: the odyssey of the sentence and the novel of Flaubert's novels. Thus, the sentence becomes, in our literature, a new object: not only *de jure,* in Flaubert's numerous declarations in this regard, but *de facto:* a sentence by Flaubert is immediately identifiable, not by its "air," its "color," or some turn of phrase habitual to the writer—which we might say of any author—but because it always presents itself as a separate, finite object, which we might almost call transportable, though it never joins the aphoristic model, for its unit does not abide by the closure of its content, but by the evident project which has established it as an object: Flaubert's sentence is a *thing.*

As we have seen apropos of Flaubert's corrections, this thing has a history, and this history, issuing from the very structure of the language, is inscribed in every sentence by

---

[1] "I'd rather die like a dog than rush my sentence through, before it's ripe" (1852).—"I only want to write three more pages . . . and find four or five sentences that I've been searching for, nearly a month now" (1853). —"My work is going very slowly; sometimes I suffer real tortures to write the simplest sentence" (1852). —"I can't stop myself, even swimming, I test my sentences, despite myself" (1876). —And especially this, which might serve as an epigraph for what has just been said about the sentence in Flaubert: "I'm going on again, then, with my dull and simple life, poor wretched thing, in which the sentences are adventures . . ." (1857).

Flaubert. His drama (his confidences authorize us to use so novelistic a word) in confronting the sentence can be articulated as follows: the sentence is an object, in it a finitude fascinates, analogous to that finitude which governs the metrical maturation of verse; but at the same time, by the very mechanism of expansion, every sentence is unsaturable, there is no structural reason to stop it here rather than there. *Let us work in order to end the sentence* (in the fashion of a line of verse), Flaubert implicitly says at each moment of his labor, of his life, while contradictorily he is obliged to exclaim unceasingly (as he notes in 1853): *It's never finished.* [1] The Flaubertian sentence is the very trace of this contradiction, experienced intensely by the writer during the countless hours when he shuts himself up with it: it is like the gratuitous arrest of an infinite freedom, in it is inscribed a kind of metaphysical contradiction: because the sentence is free, the writer is condemned not to search for the *best* sentence, but to assume *every* sentence: no god, even the god of art, can establish it in its place.

As we know, this situation was not experienced in the same way during the entire classical period. Confronting the freedom of language, rhetoric had constructed a system of surveillance (promulgating since Aristotle the metrical rules of the "period" and determining the field of corrections, where the freedom is limited by the very nature of language, i.e., on the level of substitutions and ellipses), and this system granted the writer a slight freedom by limiting his choices. This rhetorical code—or secondary code, since it transforms the freedoms of language into constraints of expression—grows moribund by the middle of the nineteenth century; rhetoric withdraws and in a sense exposes the fundamental linguistic unit, the sentence. This new object—in which the writer's freedom is

---

[1] "Ah! What discouragements sometimes, what a Sisyphean labor style is, and prose especially! *It's never finished!*" (1853).

henceforth directly invested—Flaubert discovers with an-
guish. A writer appears a little later who will make the sentence into the site of a demonstration at once poetic and linguistic: Mallarmé's *Un coup de dés* is explicitly based on the
infinite possibility of sentential expansion, whose freedom, so
burdensome for Flaubert, becomes for Mallarmé the very
meaning—a blank meaning—of *the book to come.* Henceforth
the writer's brother and guide will no longer be the master of
rhetoric but of linguistics, the one who reveals no longer
figures of discourse but the fundamental categories of language.

(1967)

Where to Begin?

Suppose that a student wants to undertake the structural analysis of a literary work. Suppose this student is sufficiently informed not to be surprised by divergencies of approach sometimes unduly united under the label *structuralism;* sufficiently sensible to know that in structural analysis there is no such thing as a canonical method comparable to that of sociology or philosophy, so that by automatically applying it to a text, that text's structure would be revealed; sufficiently courageous to anticipate and endure the errors, breakdowns, disappointments, discouragements *("what's the use?")* which the analytic journey will not fail to provoke; sufficiently free to dare exploit what structural sensibility he may possess, what intuition of multiple meanings; sufficiently dialectical, finally, to be convinced that it is not a matter of obtaining an "explanation" of the text, a "positive result" (a final signified which would be the work's truth or its determination), but quite the contrary—that it is a matter of entering, by analysis (or what resembles an analysis), into the play of the signifier, into the writing: in a word, to accomplish, by his labor, the text's *plural.* This hero—or this sage—once found, he will nonetheless encounter an operative uneasiness, a simple difficulty, which is that of any initiation: *where to begin?* For all its practical and virtually gestual appearance (what is involved is the *first gesture* one will make in the presence of the text), we can say that this difficulty is the very one which has established modern linguistics: initially suffocated by the heteroclite nature of human language, Saussure, in order to end this oppression which is actually that of the impossible beginning, decided to choose one thread, one pertinence (that of meaning), and to unravel this thread: thus was constructed a *system* of language. In the same way, although on the secondary level of discourse, the text unravels multiple and simultaneous codes, whose systematics we do not see at first, or better still: which we cannot immediately *name*. Everything concurs, in effect, to render the structures one is seeking innocent, even absent: the unraveling of the discourse, the naturalness of the sentences, the apparent equality of significant and insignificant, academic prejudices (those of "level," of "character," of "style"), the simultaneity of meanings, the capricious disappearance and reappearance of certain thematic lodes. Confronted by the textual phenomenon, experienced as a wealth and as a nature (two good reasons to ritualize them), how to discern, to grasp the first thread, how to detach the first codes? We want to approach this work problem by proposing the *first*—primary, initial—analysis of a novel by Jules Verne, *The Mysterious Island.*

I. I. Revzin writes (in *Langages*, no. 15, 1969): "In each process of elaborating the information, we can identify a certain group A of initial signals and a certain group B of final signals observed. The task of a scientific description is to explain how the transition from A to B is effected and what the links are between these two groups (if the intermediary links are too complex and escape observation, in cybernetics, we speak of a *black box*)." Confronting the novel as a "working" system of informational items, Revzin's formulation might inspire a first undertaking: to establish the two limit groups, initial and ter-

minal, then to explore by what means, through what transformations, what mobilizations, the second joins the first or diffe-
rentiates itself from it: in short, we must define the transition
from one equilibrium to another, pass through the "black
box." The notion of an initial (or final) group is, however, not
simple; all narratives do not have the fine, eminently didactic
organization of the Balzacian novel, which opens with a static,
extensively synchronic discourse, a vast motionless concourse
of initial data which we call a *tableau* (the *tableau* is a rhetorical
notion which deserves to be studied, in that it is a challenge
to the *movement* of language); in many cases, the reader is cast
in medias res; the elements of the *tableau* are scattered throughout a diegesis which begins with the first word. This is the case
with *The Mysterious Island:* the discourse takes up the story at
full tilt (moreover, it concerns a storm). In order to *arrest* the
initial *tableau,* there is henceforth only one means: to call dia-
lectically upon the final tableau (or reciprocally, depending on
the case). *The Mysterious Island* ends with two views; the first
represents the six colonists gathered on a naked rock, they will
die of want if Lord Glenarvan's yacht doesn't save them: the
second puts these same rescued colonists in a flourishing territory they have colonized in the state of Iowa; these two final
views are obviously in a paradigmatic relation: the florescence
is in opposition to the destitution, the wealth to the want; this
final paradigm must have an initial correlative, or, if it does not
(or if it has one partially), this is because there will have been
a loss, a dilution or a transformation inside the "black box";
this is what happens: the anterior correlative of the Iowan
colonization is the colonization of the island, but this correlative is identified with the diegesis itself, it is extended to everything which happens in the novel and is therefore not a "tableau"; on the other hand, the final destitution (on the rock)
symmetrically refers us to the colonists' first destitution when,
falling out of the balloon, they have all gathered on the island

which, starting from scratch (a dog collar, a grain of wheat), they will colonize; the initial tableau, by this symmetry, is henceforth determined: it is the group of *données* collected in the work's first chapters, till the moment when, Cyrus Smith being rediscovered, the colonizing personnel is complete, confronting in a pure, almost algebraic fashion the total lack of tools (*"The fire had gone out"*: thus Chapter 8 ends the novel's initial tableau. The informational system is, in short, established as a repeated paradigm *(destitution/colonization)*, but this repetition is askew: the two destitutions are "tableaux," but the colonization is a "story"; it is this disturbance which "opens" (like a first key) the process of analysis, by revealing two codes: one, which is static, refers to the Adamic situation of the colonists, exemplary in the initial tableau and in the final one; the other, which is dynamic (which does not keep its features from being semantic), refers to the heuristic labor by which these same colonists will "discover," "penetrate," "find" both the island's nature and its secret.

Once this first sorting is made, it is an easy (if not a rapid) matter gradually to refine each of the two codes which it has disclosed. The Adamic code (or rather the thematic field of the original destitution, for this field unites several codes) includes morphologically varied terms: terms of action, indices, semes, observations, commentaries. Here, for example, are two sequences of actions which are attached to it. The first inaugurates the novel: the descent of the balloon; this descent consists, so to speak, of two threads: an actional thread, on a physical model, which recounts the stages of the airship's gradual collapse (its terms are readily discernible, numerable, and structurable), and a "symbolic" thread, on which are aligned all the features which mark (using this verb in its linguistic sense) the impoverishment, or rather the deliberate spoliation, of the colonists, at the end of which, abandoned on the island, they reconvene without baggage, without tools, without property: the dumping of the gold (10,000 francs thrown out of the gondola in an attempt to gain altitude) is in this regard duly symbolic (especially since this gold is enemy gold, that of the Confederates); the same is true of the hurricane, source of the wreck, whose exceptional, cataclysmic character performs the symbolic separation from all sociality (in the Robinsonian myth, the initial storm is not only a logical element which explains the loss of the castaway but also a symbolic element which represents a revolutionary ascesis, the transformation of social man into original man). Another sequence attached to the Adamic theme is that of the first exploration, by which the colonists ascertain whether the land on which they have just been cast is an island or a continent; this sequence is constructed as an enigma and its consummation is moreover quite poetic, since only moonlight finally discloses the truth; the instance of the discourse obviously requires that this land be an island and this island be a desert one, for it is essential, for the remainder of the discourse, that matter be given to man without tools, but also without the resistance of other men: man (if he is anything but the colonist) is therefore the enemy, at once of the castaways and of the discourse; Robinson and Jules Verne's castaways have the same fear of other men, of intruders who would appear and thereby derange the process of demonstrations, the purity of the discourse: nothing human (unless within the group) must dim the brilliant conquest of the Tool (*The Mysterious Island* is the very opposite of a prophetic novel; it is a novel of the extreme past, of the first productions of the tool).

Also participants in the Adamic theme are all the marks of a gratifying Nature: this is what we might call the Edenic code (*Adam/Eden:* a curious phonetic homology). The Edenic gift takes three forms: first, the very nature of the island is perfect, "fertile, agreeable in its aspects, varied in its productions"; next, it always supplies the necessary substance *at the appointed site:* do they want to catch birds on lines? Then *right there, on the spot,* there are creepers for lines, thorns for hooks, worms for bait; finally, when the colonists are laboring within this nature, they experience no fatigue, or at least this fatigue is *dispatched* by the discourse: this is the third form of the Edenic gift: the omnipotent discourse is identified with a gratifying Nature, it facilitates, euphorizes, reduces time, fatigue, difficulty; cutting down an enormous tree, an enterprise undertaken virtually without tools, is "liquidated" in a sentence; it would be necessary (in the course of an earlier analysis) to insist upon this *grace* which the Vernean discourse spreads over every undertaking; for on the one hand, this is just the contrary of what happens in Defoe; in *Robinson Crusoe* labor is not only exhausting (for then a word would suffice to say so) but even defined in its difficulty by the elaborate accounting of the days and weeks necessary in order to accomplish (alone) the slightest transformation: how much time, how many movements to shift, a little each day, a heavy canoe! here the function of the discourse is to show labor in slow motion, to restore its time value (which is its very alienation); and on the other hand, we see clearly the omnipotence, at once diegetic and ideological, of the instance of the discourse: Vernean euphemism permits the discourse to advance rapidly, in the appropriation of Nature, from problem to problem and not from effort to effort; it transcribes at once a promotion of knowledge and a censure of work: this is really the idiolect of the "engineer" (Cyrus Smith), of the technocrat, master of science, bard of transforming labor at the very moment when, entrusting it to others, he conjures it away; Vernean discourse, by its ellipses, its euphoric flights, dismisses time, effort, in a word, labor, to the nothingness of the unnamed: work flees, flows away, is lost in the interstices of the sentence.

Another subcode of the Adamic theme: colonization. This word is naturally ambiguous *(vacation colony, insect colony, penal colony, colonialism);* here the castaways are colonists, but they colonize only the desert, a virgin nature: every social instance is modestly erased from this diagram, in which it is a matter of transforming the earth without the mediation of any slavery: cultivators, but not colonizers. In the inventory of codes, we will nonetheless be interested to note that interhuman relationships, discreet and conventional as they are, occur in a colonial problematics, however remote; among the colonists, labor (even if they all put their hands to the plow) is hierarchically divided (the leader and the technocrat: Cyrus; the hunter: Spilett; the heir: Herbert; the specialized worker: Pencroff; the servant: Nab; the convict relegated to brute colonization, that of the herds: Ayrton); further, the black man, Nab, is a slave by essence, not in that he is "mistreated" or even "distanced" (quite the contrary: the book is humanitarian, egalitarian), or even in that his labor is inferior, but in that his psychological "nature" is of an animal order: intuitive, receptive, knowledgeable by instinct and premonition, he forms a group with the dog Top: this is the inferior moment of the scale, the bottom of the pyramid at whose top is enthroned the omnipotent Engineer; finally, we must not forget that the argument's historical horizon is of a colonial order: it is the War of Secession which, pursuing the castaways, determines and postpones a new colonization, magically purged (by the virtues of the discourse) of any alienation (it will be noted in this regard that Robinson Crusoe's adventure also has for its origin a colonial problem, a trade in black slaves by which Robinson is to get rich, transplanting them from Africa to the sugar plantations of Brazil: the myth of the desert island is based on a very real problem: how to cultivate without slaves?); and when the colonists, having lost their island, establish a new colony in America, it is in Iowa, a Western territory whose natural inhabitants, the Sioux, are as magically "absented" as any native of the Mysterious Island.

The second code which (to begin) we must unreel is that of clearing the ground; to it will be attached all the (many) features which mark both a breach and.a revelation of Nature (so as to make it *yield*, to endow it with a *profitability*). This code includes two subcodes. The first implies a transformation of Nature by means which are, so to speak, *natural:* knowledge, work, character; it is a question here of *discovering* Nature, of finding the means which lead to its exploitation: whence the "heuristic" code; it involves from the start a symbolics: that of "drilling," of "explosion," in a word, as has been said, of a breach: Nature is a crust, minerality is an essential substance to which corresponds the Engineer's function, his endoscopic energy: one must "blow up" in order to "see inside," one must "tear open" in order to liberate compressed riches: a Plutonian novel, *The Mysterious Island* mobilizes an intense telluric imagination (intense because ambivalent): the depths of the earth are at once a shelter which is conquered (Granite House, the *Nautilus*'s subterranean creek) and the concealment of a destructive energy (the volcano). It has justly been suggested (by Jean Pommier, apropos of the seventeenth century) that we study period metaphors; doubtless Vernean Plutonism is linked to the technical tasks of the industrial century: generalized breaching of the earth, of the *tellus*, by dynamite, for the exploitation of mines, the opening of highways, railroads, bridgeheads: the earth opens in order to give up its iron (a Vulcanic, igneous substance which Eiffel, notably, substitutes for stone, an ancestral substance which is "culled" on earth's surface), and this iron completes the breaching of the earth, permitting the construction of instruments of communication (bridges, rails, stations, viaducts).

The (Plutonian) symbolics are articulated on a technological theme, that of the tool. The tool, born of a reductive thought (equivalent to language and to matrimonial exchange, as Lévi-Strauss and Jakobson have observed), is itself essentially an agent of reduction: Nature (or Providence) gives the seed or the match (discovered in the child's pocket), the colonists reduce them; the examples of this reduction are numerous in *The Mysterious Island:* the tool produces the tool, according to a power which is that of number; the reducing number, whose generating virtue Cyrus carefully analyzes, is at once a magic *("There is always a way of doing everything"),* a reason (the combinatory number is precisely called a *ratio:* accountancy and *ratio* are identified etymologically and ideologically), and a safeguard (thanks to this number we do not start again from zero after each hand, each shot, or each trick, as in gambling). The code of the tool is articulated in turn around a theme at once technological (the transmutation of matter), magical (metamorphosis), and linguistic (the generation of signs), which is that of *transformation.* Although always scientific, justified according to the terms of the academic code (physics, chemistry, botany, lesson of things), transformation is always constructed as a surprise and often as a (temporary) enigma: into what can we transform seals? Answer (delayed, according to the laws of suspense): forge bellows and candles: the discourse (and not only science, which is here only to guarantee it) requires, on the one hand, that the two terms of the operation, the original substance and the object produced, the seaweed and the nitroglycerin, be as remote as possible, on the other hand, that according to the very principle of *bricolage,* every natural or given object be drawn from its *"Dasein"* and deflected toward an unexpected destination: the balloon canvas, multifunctional insofar as it is a cast-off (from the wreck), is transformed into windmill blades. We realize how close this code—which is a perpetual introduction of new, unexpected classifications—is to linguistic operations: the Engineer's transforming power is a verbal power, for both consist in combining elements (words, materials) in order to produce new systems (sentences, objects) and both draw for this upon very sure codes (language, knowledge), whose stereotypical *données* do not preclude a poetic (and poietic) return. Moreover, we can add to the transformational code (which is at once linguistic and demiurgic) a subcode whose features are abundant—that of nomination. Scarcely have they reached the summit of the mountain which gives them a panoramic view of their island than the colonists make haste to map it out, i.e., to draw it and to name its features; this first act of intellection and of appropriation is an act of language, as if all the island's chaotic substance, object of future transformations, acceded to the status of functional reality only through the net of language; in short, by mapping their island, i.e., their reality, the colonists merely fulfill the very definition of language as a "mapping" of reality.

The dis-covery of the island, as we have said, sustains two codes, the first of which is heuristic, a group of Nature-transforming features and models. The second code, much more conventional from the novelistic viewpoint, is hermeneutic; from it come the various enigmas (about ten) which justify the work's title *(The Mysterious Island)* and whose solution is delayed until Captain Nemo's final call. This code has been studied on the occasion of another text, Balzac's *Sarrasine,* and we can observe here that the formal terms will recur in *The Mysterious Island:* position, thematization, formulation of the enigma, various delaying terms (which defer the answer), unveiling-deciphering. Heuristics and hermeneutics are very close, since in both cases the island is the object of a disclosure: as Nature, its wealth must be wrested from it; as Nemo's habitat, its providential host must be deciphered; the entire work is constructed on a banal proverb: *help yourself,* labor alone to domesticate matter, *heaven will help you,* Nemo, having recognized your human excellence, will act toward you as a god. These two convergent codes mobilize two different (though complementary) symbolic systems: the breaching of nature, its subjection, domestication, transformation, the exercise of skill and knowledge (even more, as has been said, than of labor) refer to the refusal of an inheritance, to a symbolics of the Son; Nemo's action, in truth endured with some impatience by the adult Son (Cyrus), implies a symbolics of the Father (analyzed by Marcel Moré in his *Le très curieux Jules Verne*): though a singular father, a singular god, this, whose name is No One.

Our first "unraveling" will seem much more thematic than formalist: yet this is the methodological freedom which must be assumed: we cannot *begin* the analysis of a text (since that is the problem which has been raised) without taking a first semantic view (of its content), either thematic or symbolic or ideological. The (immense) work which then remains to do consists in following the first codes, in discerning their terms, in sketching the sequences, but also in positing other codes, which will appear in the perspective of the first ones. In short, if we grant ourselves the right to start from a certain *condensation* of meaning (as we have done here), it is because the movement of analysis, in its endless process, is precisely to explode the text, the first cloud of meanings, the first image of content. The stake of structural analysis is not the text's truth but its *plural;* the task, therefore, cannot consist in starting from form in order to perceive, illumine, or formulate content (there would then be no need of a structural method), but quite the contrary, in dissipating, deferring, reducing, dissolving the first content under the action of a formal science. Analysis will find its profit in this movement, which gives it both the means of starting an analysis from several familiar codes and the right to drop these codes (to transform them) by advancing, not into the text (which is always simultaneous, voluminous, stereographic), but into its own labor.

(1970)

Fromentin:
Dominique

A whole minor mythology sustains Fromentin's *Dominique;* the work is solitary twice over, since it is its author's sole novel, and since this author was not even a writer, but rather a painter; this discreet autobiography is considered one of the most general analyses of love's crisis; literarily (I mean: in the manuals of literature), we note this further paradox: at the height of the positivist and realist period (*Dominique* comes in 1862), Fromentin produces a work which passes for a major novel of psychological analysis. All of which brings it about that *Dominique* is institutionally consecrated (as for knowing who reads it, that is another matter) as a singular masterpiece: Gide put it among the ten famous books to be taken to a desert island (though what would you do there with this novel, in which no one ever eats or makes love?).

Dominique is, in fact, a punctilious novel, in which we recognize the founding values of a so-called bourgeois ideology, subsumed under an idealist psychology of the subject. This subject fills the whole book, which derives from him its unity, its continuity, its revelation; for convenience's sake, he says *I,* mingling—like every subject of bourgeois culture—his discourse and his consciousness, priding himself on this confusion under the name of *authenticity* (*Dominique*'s form is a "confession"); furnished with a transparent discourse and a consciousness without secrets, the subject can analyze himself at length: he has no unconscious, only recollections: memory is the sole form of dream known to French literature of this period; and even this memory is always "constructed": it is not an association, an irruption (as it will be in Proust), but a recall (yet in Fromentin—and this is one of his charms—anecdotal reconstruction of the incident is often overwhelmed by the insistent, effusive recollection of a moment, a place). This pure subject lives in a world without triviality: everyday objects exist for him only if they can belong to a scene, a "composition"; they never have an instrumental existence, still less do they transcend such instrumentality to disturb the thinking subject, as will happen in later novels (Fromentin, nonetheless, would have been capable of trivial inventions: witness that bouquet of rhododendrons, their roots wrapped in wet cloth, absurd gift from the future husband to his young fiancée). Finally, according to standard classical psychology, every one of the subject's adventures must have a meaning, which is generally the way in which it comes to an end: *Dominique* involves a moral lesson, a so-called lesson in wisdom: repose is one of the rare possible felicities, one must have the wit to limit oneself, romantic daydreams are blameworthy, etc.: the pure subject ends by prudently exploiting his lands and his peasants. Such is more or less what we might call *Dominique*'s ideological dossier (the word is a trifle judiciary, but perhaps we must employ it: literature is on trial).

This dossier is rather grim, but fortunately that is not all there is to *Dominique*. Not that Fromentin is to any degree revolutionary (either in politics or in literature); his novel is unfailingly docile, conformist, even pusillanimous (if we think of all that our modernity has liberated since), yoked to its heavy psychological signified, captive of a "proper" utterance, outside of which the signifier, the symbol, pleasure itself can scarcely spread. At least, by virtue of the very ambiguity of all writing, this ideological text includes certain interstices; perhaps it is possible to remodel this great idealist novel in a more material, more materialistic fashion: let us draw from the text at least all the polysemy it can yield.

Dominique's "subject" (in French we have a delicious ambiguity which is less apparent in English: the "subject" of a book is at once the speaker and what is spoken of: subject and object), *Dominique*'s subject is Love. Yet a novel can be defined by its "subject" only in a purely institutional fashion (in a library file, for instance). Even more than its "subject," a fiction's site can be its truth, because it is at the level of the site (scenes, odors, breezes, coenesthesias, weather) that the signifier is most readily articulated: the site may well be the figure of desire, without which there can be no text. In this regard, *Dominique* is not a love story but a novel of the Countryside. Here the Countryside is not only a setting (occasion of descriptions which doubtless constitute the most penetrating, the most modern element in the book) but the object of a passion ("what I can call my passion for the countryside," the narrator says: and if he permits himself to speak in this way, it is because it is really a passion which is involved, in the amorous sense of the word). The passion for the Countryside gives the discourse its basic metaphor, the autumn, in which can be read at once the melancholy of a character, the despair of an impossible love, the resignation the hero imposes on himself, and the docility of a life which, the storm once past, flows infallibly toward winter, toward death; it also gives the discourse its metonymies, i.e., certain cultural links so well known, so sure of their effect, that the Countryside becomes in a sense the obligatory site of certain identifications: first of all, the Countryside is Love, the adolescent crisis (associated, in how many novels, with the summer vacation, with youth in the provinces): a link favored by the metaphoric analogy of spring and desire, of sap and seminal liquor, of vegetal efflorescence and pubertal explosion (this is how we read the adolescent Dominique's wild excursion to the vicinity of his school town, one April Thursday); Fromentin has exploited this cultural link quite thoroughly: the Countryside is for his hero Love's eidetic site: a space eternally fated to contract and reabsorb him. Next, the Countryside is Memory, the place where there occurs a certain ponderation of time, a delicious (or painful) heeding of recollection; and insofar as the Countryside is also (and sometimes chiefly) the place of residence, a room there becomes a kind of temple of remembrance. Dominique, by a thousand notches and inscriptions, here practices "that mania for dates, figures, symbols, hieroglyphs" which makes Les Trembles into a tomb covered with commemorative seals. Lastly, the Countryside is Narrative; in it we can speak without a time limit, we confide ourselves to it, we confess to it; insofar as Nature is reputed to be silent, nocturnal (at least, in that post-romanticism to which Fromentin belongs), it is the neutral substance out of which can rise a pure, infinite discourse. Site of meaning, the Countryside is opposed to the City, site of noise; we know how much, and how bitterly, in *Dominique,* the City is discredited; Paris is a producer of *noise,* in the cybernetic sense of the word: when Dominique visits the capital, the meaning of his love, of his failure, of his perseverance, is jammed; in contrast to which the Countryside constitutes an intelligible space where life can be read in the form of a destiny. This may be why the Countryside, more than Love, is the real "subject" of *Dominique:* in the Countryside we understand why we live, why we love, why we fail (or rather, we resolve to understand nothing of all this, ever, but this very resolution soothes us like a supreme act of intelligence); we take refuge in it as in the maternal bosom, which is also death's embrace: Dominique returns to Les Trembles on the same disordered impulse which leads the gangster in *The Asphalt Jungle* to escape the city and come to die at the gate of the country house he had once started from. Curiously, the love story Fromentin tells may leave us cold; but his desire for the countryside touches us: Les Trembles, Villeneuve at night, make us envious.

This ethereal novel (its sole sensual action is a kiss) is quite brutally a class novel. We must not forget that Fromentin, whose wounded passion and romantic disenchantment are unfailingly promulgated by histories of literature, was very well integrated into Second Empire society: received in Princess Mathilde's salon, a guest of Napoleon III at Compiègne, a member of the jury of the Universal Exposition of 1867, he belonged to the delegation which inaugurated the Suez Canal in 1869; which is to say that, as a civil person, he was by no means so separated from the historical life of his age as his hero, who apparently develops in sites as socially abstract as the City and the Countryside. As a matter of fact, in Fromentin's work, the Countryside, when we consider it a little more closely, is a socially "heavy" site. *Dominique* is a reactionary novel: the Second Empire is that moment of French history when a major industrial capitalism developed with the violence of a conflagration; in this irresistible movement, the Countryside, whatever electoral contribution its peasants made to Napoleonic fascism, could only represent an already anachronistic site: refuge, dream, asociality, depoliticization, here a whole falling off of History was transformed into an ideological value. *Dominique* stages in a very direct way (though through an indirect language) all the misfits of the great capitalist promotion, summoned, in order to survive, to transform into a glorious solitude the abandonment in which History leaves them ("I was alone, last of my race, last of my rank," the hero says). In this novel there is only one character who is endowed with ambition and who seeks, through certain

antique phrases whose noble disinterestedness designates by
denial the violence of his greed, to join the race for power:
Augustin, the tutor: he has no family name, he is a bastard, a
good romantic condition for being ambitious; he hopes to ar-
rive by politics, the sole means of power which the age concedes to those who possess neither factories nor stocks; but the
others belong to a disappointed class: Olivier, the pure aristo-
crat, ends by committing suicide, or, what is still more symbolic, by disfiguring himself (he even bungles his suicide: the
aristocracy is discountenanced); and Dominique, also an aris-
tocrat, flees the City (joint emblem of worldliness, finance, and
power), and decays to the point of becoming a gentleman-
farmer, i.e., a petty exploiter: a decay which the entire novel
is concerned to consecrate under the name of wisdom, pru-
dence, obedience—*sagesse*, which we must not forget consists
of exploiting one's lands and one's workmen thoroughly; *sagesse* is exploitation without expansion. It follows that Dominique de Bray's social position is at once moral and reactionary, sublimated in the features of a benevolent patriarchy: the
husband is an idle man, he hunts and novelizes his memories;
the wife keeps the accounts; he strolls among the hired laborers, bent at their task and bending even lower to greet the
master; her task is to purify property by distributions of be-
nevolence ("She kept the keys of the pharmacy, of the linen
closet, of the woodshed, the vine shoots," etc.): a complex
association: on one side the book (the novel) and exploitation;
on the other the books (of accounts) and charity, "all this quite
simply, not even as a servitude, but as a duty of position, of
fortune and of birth." The "simplicity" which the first narrator (who is more or less Fromentin himself) attributes to the
language of the second is obviously no more than the cultural
artifice by which it is possible to naturalize class behavior; this
theatrical "simplicity" (theatrical because we are *told it*) is like
the varnish under which are assembled the rituals of culture:

the practice of the Arts (painting, music, poetry serve as references for Dominique's great love) and the style of interlocution (the characters speak to each other in that strange language which we might call "Jansenist style," whose phrases are the product—whatever the object to which they are applied, love, philosophy, psychology—of Latin composition assignments and religious tracts; for instance: "withdraw into the effacement of one's province," which is a confessor's style). The high language is not merely a way of sublimating the materiality of human relations; it creates these relations themselves: all of Dominique's love for Madeleine results from the anterior Book; this is a familiar theme of the literature of love, ever since Dante made the passion of Paolo and Francesca depend on that of Lancelot and Guinevere; Dominique is amazed to find his story in the book of others; he does not know that that is where it comes from.

Then is the body absent from this novel, which is at once social and moral (two reasons for expelling it)? Not at all; but it returns to it by a path which is never directly that of Eros: the path of pathos, a kind of sublime language which we find elsewhere in the novels and paintings of French romanticism. The gestures are deflected from their corporeal field, immediately assigned (by a haste which indeed resembles a fear of the body) to an ideal signification: what could be more carnal than to kneel before the beloved woman (i.e., to lie at her feet and, so to speak, *under her*)? In our novel, this erotic commitment is never made except for the "movement" (a word which all of classical civilization has continually shifted from body to soul) of a moral effusion, the plea for pardon; by speaking to us, apropos of Madeleine, of a "movement of an outraged woman which I shall never forget," the narrator pretends not to know that the "outraged" gesture is merely a refusal of the body (whatever its motives, here very deceptive, since, in fact, Madeleine desires Dominique: this movement is nothing more than a denial). In modern terms, we would say that in Fromentin's text (summarizing, moreover, a whole language of the period), the signifier is immediately *stolen* by the signified.

Yet this signifier (this body) returns, as it must, precisely where it has been conjured away. It returns because the love which is here narrated in a sublime mode (of reciprocal renunciation) is *at the same time* treated as a disease. Its appearance is that of a physical crisis; it paralyzes and exalts Dominique like a philter: is he not in love with the first person he meets during his wild walk, i.e., in a state of crisis (having drunk the philter), just as in a folk tale? A thousand remedies are sought for this disease, which it resists (moreover, here, too, these are caste remedies, the kind that might be imagined in the pharmacopoeia of witches: "He advised me to cure myself," Dominique says about Augustin, "but by means which he regarded as the only ones worthy of me"); and once the crisis is (imperfectly) past, what is needed is rest ("I am very tired . . . I need rest")—for which one sets out for the country. Yet since what we are concerned with here is an incomplete or false nosography, the core of the trouble is never named: notably, sex. *Dominique* is a novel without sex (the logic of the signifier says that this absence is already inscribed in the ambiguity of the name which gives the book its title: Dominique is a double name: masculine and feminine); everything builds up, occurs, and concludes *outside the skin;* in the course of the story, there are only two moments of physical contact, and we can imagine what power of combustion they draw from the sensuously void milieu in which they intervene: Madeleine, engaged to Monsieur de Nièvres, rests "her two ungloved hands in the count's" (the *ungloved* hand possesses an erotic value much utilized by Pierre Klossovski): here is the entire conjugal relationship; as for the adulterous relationship (which is not fulfilled), it produces only a kiss, the one which Madeleine grants and withdraws from the narrator before leaving him forever: a whole life, a whole novel for one kiss: here sex is subjected to a *parsimonious* economy.

Blurred, decentered, sexuality goes elsewhere. Where? into emotivity, which can legally produce corporeal deflections. Castrated by morality, the man of this world (which is, by and large, the bourgeois romantic world), the male, is entitled to attitudes ordinarily reputed to be feminine: he falls to his knees (before the avenging, castrating woman, whose hand is phallicly raised in a gesture of intimidation), he faints ("I fell headlong to the floor"). Once sex is debarred, physiology becomes luxuriant; two legal (because cultural) activities become the field of erotic explosion: music (whose effects are always described excessively, as if what was involved was an orgasm ("Madeleine listened, panting . . .") and excursions (i.e., Nature: Dominique's solitary strolls, the horseback rides of Dominique and Madeleine); we might well add to these two activities, experienced in the mode of nervous erethism, a final substitute, and a worthy one: writing itself, or at least—since the period did not accept the modern distinction between speech and writing—utterance: whatever the oratorical discipline, it is certainly sexual disturbance which passes into the poetic mania of the young Dominique and into the confession of the adult man who recalls and is moved: if there are two narrators in this novel, it is because, in a sense, *expressive practice*, a substitute for unhappy, disappointed erotic activity, must be distinguished from the simple literary discourse which is subsumed by the second narrator (the first's confessor and the book's author).

In this novel there is a last transfer of the body: the desperate masochism which governs the hero's entire discourse. This notion, fallen into the public domain, is increasingly abandoned by psychoanalysis, which cannot be content with its simplicity. If we retain the word here, it is precisely by reason of its cultural value (*Dominique* is a masochist novel, in a *stereotyped* fashion), and also because this notion is readily identified with the social theme of class disappointment, which we have mentioned (that two critical discourses can be sustained in one and the same work is what is interesting: the indecisiveness of the determinations *proves* a work's literary specialty): what corresponds to the social frustration of a class (the aristocracy) which withdraws from power and buries itself *en famille* on its rural property is the doomed behavior of the two lovers; the narrative, on all its levels, from the social to the erotic, is enveloped in a great funereal drapery; this begins with the image of the wearied Father, who lags, leaning on a cane, in the wan autumn sunlight, before the espaliers of his garden; all the characters end in a living death: disfigured (Olivier), deflated (Augustin), eternally rejected (Madeleine and Dominique), mortally wounded (Julie): a notion of nothingness incessantly works in the population of *Dominique* ("He was nobody, he looked like anyone at all," etc.), without this nothingness having the slightest Christian authenticity (religion is merely a conformist decor): there is only the obsessional fabrication of failure. Love, throughout this story, these pages, is, in fact, *constructed* according to a rigorously masochist economy: desire and frustration are united in it like the two parts of a sentence, necessary in proportion to the meaning it must have: love is born in the very perspective of its failure, it cannot be named (accede to recognition) except at the moment when it is acknowledged to be impossible: "If you knew how much I love you," Madeleine says; ". . . today I can confess it, since it is the forbidden word which separates us." Love, in this prim novel, is, in fact, an instrument of torture: it approaches, wounds, burns, but does not kill; its operative function is to *render infirm . . . ;* it is a deliberate mutilation inflicted within the very field of desire: "Madeleine is lost and I love her!" exclaims Dominique; we must read the opposite: I love Madeleine because she is lost: it is loss itself, in accordance with the old myth of Orpheus, which defines love.

The obsessional character of amorous passion (as it is described in Fromentin's book) determines the structure of the love story. This structure is composite, it combines (and this impurity perhaps defines the novel) two systems: a dramatic system and a ludic system. The dramatic system accommodates a structure of crisis; its model is organic (to be born, to live, to struggle, to die); born of the encounter of a virus and a terrain (puberty, the Countryside), passion is established, and pervades; after which, it confronts the obstacle (the beloved's marriage): this is the crisis, whose resolution is here death (renunciation, retreat); in narrative terms, every dramatic structure has as its mainspring *suspense:* how will this end? Even if we know from the very first pages that "this will end badly" (and the narrator's masochism announces this to us continuously), we cannot keep ourselves from experiencing the uncertainties of an enigma (will they end by making love?); there is nothing surprising about this: reading, in fact, seems to derive from a perverse behavior (in the psychoanalytic sense of the term) and to be based on what since Freud we call the *splitting of the ego:* we know *and* we do not know how all this will end. This separation (this splitting) of knowledge and expectation is the very characteristic of tragedy: reading Sophocles, everyone knows that Oedipus has killed his father, but everyone trembles at not knowing it. In *Dominique,* the question attached to any love story, any drama of love, is doubled by an initial enigma: what is it, then, which could have turned Dominique into a man buried alive? Yet—and this is a rather complicated aspect of the novel of love—the dramatic structure is suspended at a certain moment and permits itself to be penetrated by a ludic structure: this is my name for any *motionless* structure articulated on the binary oscillation of repetition—as we find it described in the *vort/da* game of the Freudian child: once passion is established and blocked, it oscillates between desire and frustration, happiness and misery, purification and aggression, the love scene and the scene of jealousy, in a literally *interminable* manner: nothing warrants putting an end to this interplay of appeals and rejections. For the love story to end, the dramatic structure must regain the upper hand. In *Dominique*, it is the kiss, resolution of desire (and how elliptical a resolution!), which puts an end to the enigma: for henceforth we know *everything* about the two partners: the knowledge of the story has joined the knowledge of desire: the reader's "ego" is no longer split, there is nothing further to read, the novel can, the novel must, end.

In this backward-looking novel, what is most surprising is, finally, the language (that uniform layer which covers the utterance of each character and of the narrator, the book marking no idiolectal difference). This language is always *indirect;* it names things only when it can make them attain to a high degree of abstraction, to distance them beneath a crushing generality. What Augustin does, for instance, reaches the discourse only in a form which escapes all identification: "His will alone, supported by a rare good sense, by a perfect rectitude, his will worked miracles"; what miracles? This is a very curious method; a touch more here and there and it would be quite modern (it heralds what we have been able to call the negative rhetoric of a Marguerite Duras): does it not consist in making the referent unreal and, so to speak, formalizing to extremes the novel's psychologism (a procedure which might, with a little boldness, have been able to depsychologize the novel altogether)? Augustin's actions remaining buried under a carapace of allusions, the character ends by losing all corporality, reduced to an essence of Labor, of Will, etc.: Augustin is a cipher. Hence *Dominique* can be read with as much stupefaction as a medieval allegory; the allusiveness of the utterance is taken so far that the latter becomes obscure, amphigoric; we keep being told that Augustin is ambitious, but we are told only very late and in passing what the field of his exploits is, as if it were of no concern to us to know whether he wants to succeed in literature, in the theater, or in politics. Technically, this distance is that of the *summary:* there is no end to summarizing under a generic label (Love, Passion, Labor, Will, Dignity, etc.) the multiplicity of attitudes, actions, motives. The language tries to return to its so-called source, which is Essence, or, less philosophically, genre; and *Dominique* is in this indeed a novel of origins: by confining himself to abstraction, the narrator imposes on the language an origin which is not the Fact (a "realistic" view) but the Idea (an "idealistic" view). We understand better then, perhaps, the considerable ideological advantage of this continuously indirect language: it honors all the possible meanings of the word "correction": *Dominique* is a "correct" book: because it avoids any trivial representation (we never know what the characters eat, except when they are of the lower classes, vineyard laborers who are served roast goose to celebrate the harvest); because it respects the classical precepts of good literary style; because it affords nothing but a discreet effluvium of adultery: that of adultery evaded; finally, because all these rhetorical distances homologically reproduce a metaphysical hierarchy, the one which separates the soul from the body, it being understood that these two elements are separated so that their eventual encounter may constitute a dreadful subversion, a panic Offense: against taste, against morality, against language.

"I beg you," Augustin says to his pupil, "never believe those who tell you that the reasonable is the enemy of the beautiful, because it is the inseparable friend of justice and truth": this kind of sentence is virtually unintelligible today; or, if we prefer to give our astonishment a more cultural form: who could understand it, after having read Marx, Freud, Nietzsche, Mallarmé? The anachronism of *Dominique* is certain. Yet, inventorying some of the distances which compose it, I have not necessarily meant that we must not read this book; I wanted, quite the contrary, by marking out the lineaments of a powerful network, somehow to liquidate the resistances which such a novel might provoke in a modern reader, so that there might then appear, during the actual reading—like the characters of a magic writing which, having been invisible, gradually become articulate under the effect of heat—the interstices of the ideological prison in which *Dominique* is held. This heat, producing an ultimately legible writing, is, or will be, that of our pleasure. There are in this novel many corners of pleasure, which are not necessarily distinct from the alienations we have indicated: a certain incantation, produced by the eloquence of the sentences, the voluptuous delicacy of the descriptions of the countryside, as penetrating as the pleasure we take in certain romantic paintings and, more generally, as was said at the start, the hallucinatory plenitude (I should go so far as to say: the eroticism) attached to every notion of withdrawal, of repose, of equilibrium; a conformist life is loathsome when we are in a waking state, i.e., when we are speaking the necessary language of values; but in moments of fatigue, of weakness, at the height of urban alienation or of the linguistic vertigo of human relations, a dream of bygones is not impossible: the life at Les Trembles. Then all things are inverted: *Dominique* seems to us a kind of illegal book: in it we discern the voice of a demon: a costly, culpable demon, since he invites us to idleness, to irresponsibility, to home; in a word, to *sagesse*.

(1971)

Pierre Loti:
Aziyadé

The Name

In the name Aziyadé, this is what I read and what I hear: first of all the gradual explosion (like a bouquet of fireworks) of the three brightest vowels in the French alphabet (the opening of the vowels = the opening of the lips, of the senses); the caress of the *z*, the sensuous, plump palatalization of the *y*, this entire sonorous series sliding and spreading, subtle and rich; next a constellation of islands, stars, peoples, Asia, Georgia, Greece; and then a whole literature: Hugo who in his *Orientales* uses the name Albaydé, and behind Hugo all of philhellene romanticism; Loti, a traveler specializing in the East, the bard of Istanbul; the vague notion of a feminine character (some *Désenchantée*); finally the prejudice of dealing with an insipid, sweetish, old-fashioned novel: in short, from the (sumptuous) signifier to the (paltry) signified, utter disappointment. Yet, from another region of literature, someone comes and tells us we must always *reverse* the disappointment of a proper name, making this reversal into the trajectory of an apprenticeship: the Proustian narrator, starting from the phonetic glory of the Guermantes, finds in the Duchess's world something quite different from what the orange splendor of the Name had led him to suppose, and it is by *retracing* his narrator's disappointment that Proust can write his work. Perhaps we, too, can learn to disappoint the name Aziyadé in the right way and, after having slipped from the precious name to the pathetic image of an outdated novel, work our way back to the idea of a *text:* fragment of the infinite language which tells nothing but in which occurs *"something unheard-of and shadowy."*

Loti

Loti is the novel's hero (even if he has other names and even if this novel presents itself as the narrative of a reality, not of a fiction): Loti is *in* the novel (the fictive creature, Aziyadé, constantly calls her lover *Loti: "Look, Loti, and tell me . . . "*); but he is also outside it, since the Loti who has written the book in no way coincides with the hero Loti: they do not have the same identity: the first Loti is British and dies young; the second Loti, whose first name is Pierre, is a member of the Académie Française, and he has written many other books besides the account of his Turkish *amours.* Nor does the game of identities stop there: this second Loti, so well established in the world of literary commerce and honors, is not the actual, civilian author of *Aziyadé:* the latter was named Julien Viaud and happened to be a little gentleman who toward the end of his life had himself photographed in his house at Hendaye, dressed *à l'orientale* and surrounded by a whole bazaar of exotic objects (and had at least one taste in common with his hero: transvestism). It is not the pseudonym who is interesting (in literature, that is banal), but the other Loti, the one who is and is not his character, the one who is and is not the book's author: I don't think there exists one like him in literature, and his invention (by the third man, Viaud) is quite a bold stroke: for if it is a commonplace to sign the narrative of what happens to you and thereby to give your name to one of your characters (this is what occurs in any private diary), it is not one to invert the bestowal of the proper name; yet this is what Viaud has done: he has given to himself, the author, the name of his hero. So that, caught up in a network of three terms, the man who signs the book is false twice over: the Pierre Loti who guarantees *Aziyadé* is not at all the Loti who is its hero; and this guarantor *(auctor, author)* is himself fabricated, the author is not Loti but Viaud: it is all played out between a homonym and a pseudonym; what is missing, what is passed over in silence, what is wide open, is the proper name, the propriety of the name (the name which specifies and the name which appropriates). Where is the scriptor?

Monsieur Viaud is in his house at Hendaye, surrounded by his Moroccan and Japanese trash; Pierre Loti is in the Académie Française; Loti the British lieutenant died in Turkey in 1877 (at which time the other Loti was twenty-seven years old, so that he has survived the first one by sixty-six years). Of whom is this the story? Of which *subject?* In the very signature of the book, by the adjunction of this second Loti, of this third scriptor, a hole is made, a person is lost, by means much more cunning than mere pseudonomy.

What Happens?

A man loves a woman (as a poem by Heine begins); he is obliged to leave her; they both die of it. Is this really what *Aziyadé* is? Even when we add to this anecdote its circumstances and its setting (it takes place in Turkey, at the time of the Russo-Turkish war; neither the man nor the woman is free, they are separated by differences—of nationality, religion, manners, etc.), we have said nothing about the book, for it is consumed, paradoxically enough, only in the simple contact of the banal story. What is recounted is not an adventure but *incidents:* we must take the word in as slight, as modest, a sense as possible. The incident—already much weaker than the accident (but perhaps more disturbing)—is simply *what falls* gently, like a leaf, on life's carpet; it is that faint, fugitive crease given to the fabric of days; it is what can be *just barely* noted: a kind of notation degree zero, precisely what is needed to be able to write *something.* Loti—or Pierre Loti—excels in these insignificances (which are in perfect agreement with the book's ethical project, the account of a dip into the intemporal substance of the outdated): a walk, a wait, an excursion, a conversation, a ceremony, a winter evening, a sinister party, a fire, the arrival of a cat, etc.: all that presence of which our expectation appears to constitute an absence; but also all that external (externalized) emptiness which constitutes happiness.

Nothing

In other words, *nothing* happens. Yet this *nothing* must be said. How do you say: *nothing?* Here we are faced with a great paradox of writing: *nothing* can be said only as *nothing; nothing* is perhaps the only word in the language which admits of no periphrase, no metaphor, no synonym, no substitute; for to say *nothing* in any other way than by its pure denotation (the word *nothing*) is immediately to fill the nothing, to belie it: like Orpheus, who loses Eurydice by turning back to look at her, *nothing* loses a little of its meaning each time it is set forth (set back). Hence we must cheat. *Nothing* can be caught up in discourse only obliquely, on the bias, by a kind of deceptive allusion; thus, Loti produces a thousand tenuous notations whose object is neither an idea nor a sentiment nor a fact, but simply, in the widest sense of the term, *the weather outside.* This "subject," which in everyday conversations the world over certainly occupies first place, deserves some study: despite its apparent futility, does it not articulate the void of discourse across which human society is constituted? To speak *about the weather* was initially a positive communication, the information required by the farmer's practice, whose harvest depends on the weather; but in urban relations, this subject is a void one, and this void is the very meaning of interlocution: we speak of the weather *in order to say nothing*, i.e., in order to tell the other we are speaking to him, in order to tell him nothing but this: I am speaking to you, you exist for me, I want to exist for you (hence it is a falsely superior attitude to make fun of the weather as a subject); further, however empty the "subject," the weather refers to a kind of complex existence of the world (of what is) which unites place, decor, light, temperature, coenesthesia, and which is that fundamental mode according to which my body is here, feeling itself exist (not to mention the happy or melancholy connotations of the weather, depending on whether it favors our daily plans); this is why what the weather happened to be (in Salonika, in Constantinople, in Eyoub), which Loti tirelessly records, has a multiple function as writing: it permits the discourse to *stand* without saying anything (by saying *nothing*), it disappoints or deceives meaning, and, coined into a few adjacent notations (*"oats were sprouting between the black paving stones . . . everywhere you could smell the warm air and the sweet odor of the month of May"*), it allows us to refer to some *Dasein* of the world, something primary, natural, incontestable, and in-significant (where meaning begins is where interpretation begins as well, which is where the combat is). Hence we understand the complicity established between these minor notations and the very genre of the private diary (Amiel's is full of the weather on the shores of Lake Geneva in the last century): since its intention is only to express the *nothing* of my life (managing not to construe it as Fate), the diary makes use of that special body whose "subject" is merely the contact of my body and of its envelope and which we call *the weather outside.*

Anacoluthon

The weather outside serves for something else (or for the same thing): to break meaning, to break *construction* (of the world, the dream, the narrative). In rhetoric, we call this rupture of construction anacoluthon. For example, in his corvette cabin, off Salonika, Loti dreams of Aziyadé, whose long braid of brown hair is being handed to him by Samuel; he is wakened for the watch and the dream is interrupted; nothing more is said, to conclude, than this: *"It rained in torrents that night, and I was soaked."* Thus the dream discreetly loses all meaning, even the meaning of meaninglessness; the rain (the notation of the rain) smothers that flash of meaning Shakespeare speaks of: meaning, broken, is not destroyed, it is—that rare, difficult thing—*exempted.*

The Two Friends

In his adventure with Aziyadé, Lieutenant Loti is helped by two servants, by two friends, Samuel and Achmet. Between these two affections, *"there is an abyss."*

Achmet has tiny eyes; Samuel's are very gentle. Achmet is original, generous, he is the friend of hearth and home, the intimate; Samuel is the boat boy, the attendant of the floating bed, he is the messenger, friend of the waves. Achmet is the man of Islamic fixity; Samuel is a mixture of Jew, Italian, Greek, and Turk; he is the man of mixed language, of the Sabir, the *lingua franca.* Achmet is Aziyadé's knight and espouses her cause; Samuel is her jealous rival. Achmet is on the side of virility *("built like Hercules");* Samuel is feminine, he casts wheedling glances and is clean as a tabby cat. Samuel is infatuated with Loti; this is not articulated, of course, though it is signified *("His hand trembled in mine and squeezed it more than would have been necessary. 'Che volete,' he said in a dark and troubled voice, 'che volete mi?' What do you want with me? . . . Something unheard-of and shadowy had flashed through poor Samuel's mind—in the East, anything is possible!—and then he buried his face in his arms and stood there, terrified of himself, motionless and trembling . . .").* A motif appears here—which is visible in other places as well: no, *Aziyadé* is not altogether a novel for well-brought-up girls, it is also a minor Sodomite epic, studded with allusions to *something unheard-of and shadowy.*

The paradigm of the two friends is therefore clearly formulated (the friend/the lover), but it has no consequence: it is not *transformed* (into action, into plot, into drama): the meaning remains somehow indifferent. This novel is an almost motionless discourse, which posits meanings but does not resolve them.

The Forbidden

Strolling through Constantinople, Lieutenant Loti passes along endless walls, linked high above him by a little gray marble bridge. It is the same with the Forbidden: it is not only what we follow endlessly but also what communicates above us: an enclosure from which we are excluded. Another time, Loti makes his way, in a venture of immense daring, into the second interior courtyard of the holy mosque of Eyoub, fiercely forbidden to Christians; he raises the leather curtain which closes off the sanctuary, but we know that inside mosques there is nothing at all: all this trouble, all this transgression in order to verify a void. Here again, perhaps, the same is true of the Forbidden: a heavily proscribed space whose heart is nonetheless *aseptic.*

Loti I (the book's hero) confronts many forbidden things: the harem, adultery, the Turkish language, the Islamic religion, Oriental dress; how many enclosures he must find the password into, imitating those who are permitted to enter them! The difficulties of the enterprise are often emphasized, but curiously enough, how they are surmounted is scarcely mentioned. If we imagine what a seraglio might have been (and so many stories exist to tell us of their fierce closure), if we recall for a moment how difficult it is to speak a foreign language such as Turkish without betraying one's character as a foreigner, if we consider how rare it is to dress exotically without seeming to be in disguise, how can we admit that Loti could have lived for months with a woman of the harem, spoken Turkish in a few weeks, etc.? We are told nothing about the concrete means of the enterprise—which would elsewhere have constituted the essentials of the novel (of the plot).

This is, no doubt, because for Loti II (the book's author) the Forbidden is an idea; it matters little, in short, if the Forbidden is violated; the important thing, endlessly expressed, is to posit it, and to posit oneself in relation to it. *Aziyadé* is the necessary name of the Forbidden, the pure form under which a thousand social transgressions can be accounted for, from adultery to pederasty, from irreligion to grammatical errors.

The Pale Debauch

The pale debauch is that of the earliest hours of the morning, when a whole night of erotic dawdling comes to an end (*"The pale debauch often kept me out in the streets well into the daylight hours"*). Waiting for Aziyadé, Lieutenant Loti knows many such nights, filled by *"strange things," "a strange prostitution," "some imprudent adventure,"* all experiences which certainly include "the vices of Sodom" for whose satisfaction appear Samuel or Izeddin-Ali, the guide, the initiator, the accomplice, the organizer of saturnalia from which women are excluded; these refined or low-class revels, to which several allusions are made, always end in the same way: Loti condemns them disdainfully, claims, but a little too late, to have no part in them (as in the case of the cemetery guard, whose advances he accepts before pitching him over a precipice; as in the case of old Kairoullah, whom he provokes into offering his twelve-year-old son, "handsome as an angel," and whom he ignominiously dismisses at dawn): a familiar stratagem of bad faith, this discourse serving retrospectively to annul the preceding orgy, which nonetheless constitutes the essential element of the message; for ultimately *Aziyadé* is *also* the story of a debauch. Constantinople and Salonika (their poetical descriptions) cover for encounters hypocritically called untoward, and for persistent cruising of young Asiatic boys; the seraglio covers for the ban on homosexuality; the young lieutenant's blasé skepticism, which he works up into theories for his Western friends, covers for the spirit of the hunt, the insatiability—or the systematic satisfaction—of desire, which permits it to sprout all over again; and Aziyadé, so gentle and pure, covers for the sublimation of these pleasures: which explains why she is so nimbly dispatched, like a moral couplet, at the end of a night, of a paragraph of "debauch": *"Then I remembered that I was in Constantinople—and that she had promised to come there."*

The Major Paradigm

"Debauch": that is the strong term of our story. The other term, the one to which this one must be in opposition, is not, I believe, Aziyadé. Counter-debauch is not purity (love, sentiment, fidelity, conjugality) but constraint, i.e., the Occident represented twice over in the form of the police commissioner. By sinking deliciously into Asiatic debauchery, Lieutenant

Loti is fleeing the *moral* institutions of his country, of his culture, of his civilization; whence the intermittent dialogue with the tiresome sister and the British friends Plumkett and Brown, both so menacingly sprightly: you can skip these letters: their function is purely structural: it is a matter of assuring desire its repellent term. But, then, Aziyadé? Aziyadé is the neutral term, the zero term of this major paradigm: discursively, she occupies the front rank; structurally, she is absent, she is the place of an absence, she is a fact of discourse, not a fact of desire. Is it really she, is it not rather Constantinople (i.e., the "pale debauch"), which Loti finally wants to choose against the *Deerhound,* against England and the politics of the great powers, the sister, the friends, the old mother, the lord and lady playing Beethoven in the salon of a *pension de famille?* Loti I seems to die of Aziyadé's death, but Loti II carries on: the lieutenant nobly dispatched, the author will go on describing cities, in Japan, in Persia, in Morocco, i.e., will go on designating and searchlighting (by emblems of discourse) the space of his desire.

Costumes

A moralist one day exclaimed: I would gladly convert, if I could wear a caftan and a djellaba! In other words: all the lies in the world if only what I wear tells the truth! I prefer my soul lie, rather than my dress! My soul for a costume! Transvestites are in hot pursuit of the truth: what most horrifies them is precisely to be *disguised:* there is a moral sensitivity to the truth of clothes, and when one possesses it, this sensitivity is very touchy: Colonel Lawrence endured many an ordeal for the right to wear the *shan.* Lieutenant Loti is a fanatic of transvestism; he costumes himself first of all for tactical reasons (as a Turk, as a sailor, as an Albanian, as a dervish), then for ethical reasons: he wants to convert, to become a Turk in essence, i.e., in costume; it is a problem of identity; and since what is abandoned—or adopted—is a total person, there must be no contagion between the two costumes, the Occidental cast-offs and the new garments; whence those sites of transformation, those transformation chambers (among the Salonikan Jewesses, or with Madame de Galata), those airtight sluices where identities are scrupulously exchanged, one dying (Loti), the other born (Arif).

This dialectic is familiar: we know that the garment does not *express* but constitutes the person; or rather, we know that the person is nothing but this desired image which the garment permits us to believe in. What, then, is the person whom Lieutenant Loti wants for himself? Without doubt that of a Turk of the old days, i.e., a man of pure desire, cut loose from the Occident and from modernism, insofar as, in the eyes of a modern Occidental, one and the other are identified with the very responsibility of living. But under the journal of Lieutenant Loti, the author Pierre Loti is writing something else: the person he wants for his character, when he lends him these fine old costumes, is the person of a pictorial being: *"To be oneself a part of this tableau so full of movement and of light,"* says the lieutenant who, dressed up as an old Turk, visits the mosques, the cafedjis, the baths, and the squares, i.e., the *tableaux* of Turkish life. Hence the goal of transvestism is *finally* (once the illusion of being is exhausted), to transform oneself into a describable object—and not into an introspectible subject. The consecration of the disguise (what belies it by dint of its success) is pictorial integration, the passage from the body into a collective writing, in a word (if we are to take it literally), *transcription:* dressed *exactly* (i.e., in a garment from which the excess of exactitude is banished), the subject dissolves himself, not by intoxication, but by Apollinism, by participation in a proportion, in a combination system. Hence a minor author, outdated and evidently unconcerned with theory (though a contemporary of Mallarmé, of Proust), brings to light the most complex of writing's logics: for wanting to be "the one who belongs to the tableau" is to write only insofar as one is written: that abolition of passive and active, of expresser and expressed, of subject and statement, in which modern writing precisely seeks to discover itself.

But Where Is the Orient?

How remote it seems, that period when the language of Islam was Turkish and not Arabic! This is because the cultural image is always fixed where the political power is: in 1877 the "Arab countries" did not exist; though vacillating (*Aziyadé*, in its way, tells us as much), Turkey was still, politically and therefore culturally, the very sign of the Orient (exoticism within exoticism: Loti's Orient includes moments of winter, of fog, of cold: it is the extremity of our Orient, censored by modern tourism). A hundred years later, i.e., in our day, what would have been Lieutenant Loti's Oriental fantasy? No doubt some Arab country, Egypt or Morocco; here the lieutenant—perhaps some young professor—would have sided against Israel, the way Loti takes up the cause of his beloved Turkey against the Russians: all this on account of Aziyadé— or of the *pale debauch.*

Whether Turkish or Maghrebi, the Orient is merely a square on the board, the emphatic term of an alternative: the Occident or *something else.* As long as the opposition is unresolved, merely subjected to forces of *temptation,* meaning functions positively: the book is possible, *it develops.* When Loti is constrained to *opt* (as is said in administrative circles), he must shift from the imaginary level to the real level, from an ethic to a status, from a way of life to a political responsibility; he must yield to the constraint of a *praxis:* meaning ceases, the book stops, for there is no longer any signifier, and the signified resumes its tyranny.

What is remarkable is that the hallucinatory investment, the *possibility* of meaning (and not its halt), what is *previous to* the decision, outside it, always occurs, it seems, with the help of a political regression: bearing on the mode of life, desire is always feudal: in a Turkey herself out of date, it is a still older Turkey that Loti seeks out, trembling: desire always proceeds toward an extreme archaism, where the greatest historical distance assures the greatest unreality, there where desire finds its pure form: that of an impossible return, that of the Impossible (but in writing it, this regression will disappear).

The Journey, the Sojourn

A fragile form serves as a transition or a passage—that neutral, ambiguous term dear to the great classifiers—between an ethical intoxication (the love of an *art of living*) and a national engagement (or, as we would say, politics): this is the *sojourn* (a notion which has its administrative correspondent: *residence*); Loti knows, transposed into modern terms, the three graduated moments of all alienation: the journey, the sojourn, and naturalization; he is successively a tourist (in Salonika), a resident (in Eyoub), a national (officer in the Turkish Army). Of these three moments, the most contradictory is the sojourn (the residence): here the subject no longer has the tourist's ethical irresponsibility (who is simply a national on tour), but does not yet have the citizen's responsibility (civilian, political, military); he is posited between two strong statuses, and this intermediary position, nonetheless, *lasts*—is defined by the very slowness of its development (whence, in Loti's sojourn at Eyoub, a mixture of eternity and precariousness: this "ceaselessly harks back" and this "is endlessly about to end"): the resident is, in short, a tourist who *repeats* his desire to remain (*"I inhabit one of the loveliest countries of the world*—words of a tourist, an amateur of tableaux, of photographs—*and my freedom is limitless"*—intoxication of the resident, whom a fine knowledge of sites, manners, and language allows to satisfy every desire without fear (this is what Loti calls: freedom).

The *sojourn* has its own substance: it makes the country of residence, and singularly here Constantinople, a composite space into which is condensed the substance of several great cities, an element in which the subject can *dive:* that is, sink, hide, slip away, intoxicate himself, vanish, absent himself, die to everything which is not his desire. Loti makes clear the schizoid nature of his experience: *"I no longer suffer, I no longer remember: I should pass indifferent beside those whom I once adored . . . I believe in nothing and in no one, I love no one and nothing; I have neither faith nor hope";* this is obviously the *brink* of madness, and by this residential experience, whose really untenable character we have just described, Lieutenant Loti finds himself repossessed of the magical and poetic aura of beings who have broken with society, with reason, with sentiment, with humanity: he becomes the paradoxical being who cannot be classified: this is what he is told by the dervish Hassan-Effendi, who makes Loti into the contradictory subject, the young and very learned man whom the old rhetoric used to exalt—a veritable *impossibility* of nature—under the name of *puer senilis:* having the characteristics of all ages, exempt from time because possessed of all times at once.

Drift

Were it not for its alibis (a fine philosophy of disenchantment and Aziyadé herself), this novel might be quite modern: does it not offer the same slothful contestation one finds today in the hippie movement? Loti is something of a hippie dandy:

like him, the hippies have a taste for expatriation and for transvestism. This kind of rejection or of withdrawal from the West is neither violent nor ascetic nor political: it is precisely a *drift: Aziyadé* is the novel of Drift. There exist cities of Drift: neither too big nor too new, they must have a past (like Tangier, an old international city), yet still be lively; cities in which several inner cities mingle, cities without a promotional spirit, idle cities yet not luxury cities, in which debauch reigns without taking itself seriously: such no doubt was Loti's Constantinople. The city is, then, a kind of water which both carries and carries us away far from the shore of the real: here we are motionless (withdrawn from any competition) and deported (withdrawn from any conserving order). Curiously, Loti himself speaks of the drift (a rare truly symbolic moment in this discourse without secrets): in the waters of Salonika, the boat in which Aziyadé and he make their amorous excursions is a "floating bed," "a bed that drifts" (which finds its opposite in the canoe *Maria Pia,* loaded with noisy pleasure seekers, which almost capsizes them). Is there a more voluptuous image than this one of a drifting boat? A profound image, for it unites three ideas: that of love, that of floating, and the notion that desire is a force adrift—which is why the French word for drift, *dérive,* has been offered as the best approximation, if not the best translation, of the Freudian *pulsion* (a concept which has provoked many arguments): Lieutenant Loti's drift (on the waters of Salonika, in the suburb of Eyoub, during winter evenings with Aziyadé or exploring debauchery in the cellars and cemeteries of Constantinople) is, therefore, the exact figure of his desire.

Default

Even a few years ago, during the winter, the European quarter of the city of Marrakesh was completely dead (subsequently tourism has reinvigorated it to excess); in the heat, along the broad avenues with their open but futile shops, their virtually empty café terraces, in the public gardens where here and there a man was sleeping on a rare patch of grass, one could relish that penetrating sentiment: default. Everything subsists and yet nothing belongs to anyone any more; each thing, present in its complete form, is drained of that combative tension attached to propriety; there is a loss, not of goods, but of heritage and of heirs. Such is Loti's Constantinople; alive, even lively, like a bright-colored, odorous tableau, but without owners: Turkey in its death throes (as a great power), modernism at the gates, with few defenses, and here and there the cult of the outdated, of *passé* refinement—of the past as refinement. It is this default, this historical drift, which was doubtless expressed by the Turkish word *eski* (deliciously ambiguous to French ears), cited as a favorite word by Lieutenant Loti: *"I examined the old men who surrounded me: their costumes indicated the scrupulous concern with the fashions of the good old days; everything they wore was* eski, *even their huge silver spectacles, even the lines of their ancient profiles.* Eski, *a word uttered with veneration, which means* antique *and which is applied in Turkey as much to old customs as to old forms of clothes or to old stuffs."* Just as Drift has its emblematic object in the floating bed, so Default has its thematics: the grass sprouting between the paving stones, the black cypresses cutting across the white marbles, the cemeteries (so numerous in Loti's Turkey), which are not so much sites of death as spaces of debauch, of drift.

Motives

Have I managed to say—and yet without forcing—that this old-fashioned novel—which is barely a novel at all—has something modern about it? Not only does the writing, proceeding from desire, constantly touch on the forbidden, alienate the writing subject, and baffle him; but even (this being merely the structural translation of the foregoing) the functional levels are multiple: they tremble within each other. He who speaks (Loti) is not he who writes (Pierre Loti); the utterance of the narrative emigrates, as in a hand-over-hand game, from Viaud to Pierre Loti, from Pierre Loti to Loti, then to Loti-in-disguise (Arif), to his correspondents (his sister, his British friends). As for the structure, it is double, equally narrative and descriptive; whereas ordinarily (in Balzac, for instance) the descriptions are only informative digressions, halts, here they have a propulsive force: the movement of the discourse is in the renewed metaphor which always speaks the *nothing* of Drift. And the story itself—where is it? Is it the story of an unhappy love? The odyssey of an expatriate soul? The muted, allusive narrative of a debauch *à l'orientale?* The dervish Hassan-Effendi questions: *"Will you tell us, Arif or Loti, who you are and what you have come among us to do?"* There is no answer: the journey—Loti's Turkish sojourn—is without motive and without end, it has neither why nor wherefore; it belongs to no determination, to no teleology: something which is very often pure signifier has been articulated—and the signifier is never outdated.

(1971)